Learning to Lead from

Your Spiritual Center

LEARNING TO LEAD FROM YOUR SPIRITUAL CENTER

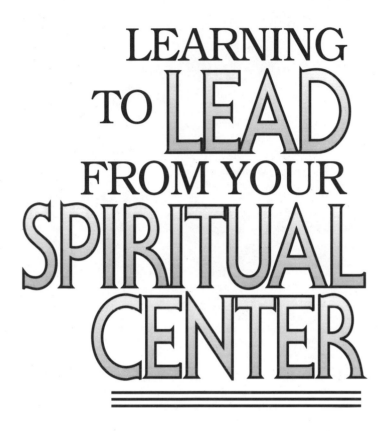

Patricia D. Brown

ABINGDON PRESS / Nashville

LEARNING TO LEAD FROM YOUR SPIRITUAL CENTER

This book is printed on recycled, acid-free paper.

ISBN 0-687-00612-0

98 99 00 01 02 03 04 05 — 10 9 8 7 6 5 4 3

MANUFACTURED IN THE UNITED STATES OF AMERICA

For my son, Christian Paul Gloddy,
as we companion the leadership journey
and enfold each other in hope and possibility.

CONTENTS

INTRODUCTION
Leadership as a Spiritual Quest

This book is about truth telling. It is about seeking to live and lead in spirit-filled ways. It is not about leadership as management or administration. It does not deal with how to get a raise or a promotion, or how to dress for success. It isn't a guide for minorities and women on how to break through the glass ceiling, as worthwhile as that would be. If you're looking for the latest on techniques of persuasion or how to organize a system, this book is not for you. If, however, you want to lead from your spiritual center, if you want to learn about leadership as a spiritual quest, read on.

Most days I strive to be a principle-centered leader working out of high morals and values. I try to live according to my religious upbringing, adhering to the rules and beliefs I was taught. On better days I live reverently, spiritually minded, in touch with the mysteries of life. I strive to walk in holiness with a loving attitude. I lean toward myself and others with a gentle spirit rather than a spirit of judgment. I am open to my own and other people's sacredness and operate out of a sense of their worth as unique persons of God.

If the truth be told (and I promised it would be), there are days when I almost lose my faith and it takes everything I have to hang on to a sliver of godliness. The last thing I want to be is holy and loving! I am as hard on other people

9

as I am on myself. My spirit is not gentle, but harsh and judging. Time and time again I've had to stop in my tracks, step away, and regain a sense of who I am. I pause to remind myself what is of primary importance for my own life and my relationships with others. It is not an easy task. This confession might surprise you, since I am a person who works, of all places, within the structure of the church. Surely, if anywhere, the church is the place where peace and love abound!

As a tenderfoot pastor serving my first parish, I was dismayed by what I found. My congregation was not a harmonious group. Instead, I discovered a fragmented community, each clique living out its belief in unnamable ways. As the novice leader, I found myself in relational triangles where I had little understanding and even less skill. My inner spirit was badly shaken.

The Woven Spirit

As I struggled with the hard questions, I was unsettled, questioning the validity of my calling to this work. Here began my journey. How could I be a spirit-centered leader in the midst of such struggle and conflict? How could I keep myself spiritually healthy so as to bring good and not harm to those whom I wished to serve? And how could I then share with congregants and others from all walks of life who wanted to lead in spirit-centered ways? I set out to find some answers. The classes I took on techniques in conflict resolution and problem solving have changed my life. Supervisory time spent understanding institutional family systems and relational dynamics revolutionized my approach. The time I spent reading books and articles about organizations and time management was not wasted. All of these gems of knowledge and skill help me to be the best leader I can be.

Yet in my search I uncovered a lesson far more precious. I found a pearl of great price! I discovered a wonderful secret: Central to my leadership is the nurturing and formation of my spirit. It is a spirit not closeted or closed off to itself, but intricately woven throughout my relationship with God, who is the Divine Center, and therefore ultimately woven to others. As I care for my spiritual well-being, I have come to realize that what I offer as a leader first arises from who I am. Leadership is not something "out there," somehow separate from me. If I am to lead in ways that evidence my faith and do not betray those I have been entrusted to serve, I must lead from a spirit-filled center.

Since my initial "baptism by fire," I have worked in other settings: as a hospital chaplain, a clinical pastoral supervisor, an executive on a major national church board, and, currently, as director of spiritual life for a large regional church body. In each place I found the same plight in leadership—leaders who fail to care for their own spiritual well-being. The failure of leaders to deal with their own souls, their inner life, is deeply troubling not only for themselves but also for other persons in the misery they cause. The destructive consequences from leaders who fail to work out of a deep sense of their inner self are staggering.

Have you ever witnessed this in your office, congregation or parish, volunteer service, or corporation? In settings where workers are irritable and people are defensive, previously motivated staffs close down. Trust levels are lowered, and walls are constructed. Only when leaders begin to nurture their own spirits will they be able to give the sustaining leadership needed for difficult, stressful times.

Working from Our Lighted Spirit

Leaders have a particular responsibility to know what is going on inside their souls. For leaders, this means taking the journey in and down. As they become fully awake, they come to know and understand what it is within that betrays them and those they strive to serve. If they do not work from their own lighted spirits, they will work from

11

their darkness, and that darkness will torrentially rain upon those they are to lead.

Five affirmations need to be in place if leaders are to lead in spirit-centered ways.

- I am a person of worth and holiness.
- I am a lover who lives out my love in mutuality, connectedness, and community.
- I am empowered, living God's will as I co-create with others.
- I not only survive but also thrive with the vision of wholeness before me.
- I can learn to lead from a new spiritual center.

Let's not be fooled. None of these affirmations is easy to live out. The truth is that we who wish to lead from a new spiritual center are once again working to uncover the inner journey. How? Through Spiritwork. Spiritwork is opening oneself to God's work within. This sacred presence empowers us to lead in ways far more effective than we ever dreamed. Spiritwork is deeply important, especially over the long haul. It is more important than any meeting, task, or project we undertake. Five spiritworks that spirit-led leaders can put in place are:

- integrating ourselves
- reaching intimacy
- connecting body and spirit
- seeking soulful souls
- naming reality.

As we work to develop or restore our inner life with God, we find new spirit-minded energy to live and lead as holy people. We will walk gently with ourselves and others. May today be your better day!

12

Changing the World
by Changing Me

O ne night I had a dream that I was standing in a tall steeple of a church overlooking a large city. As far as I could see, there were other big steeples and churches made of boulders and gray concrete and faded brick. But none as big as the one I was in. I felt alienated by what I saw. You see, I remembered that I was a child of the mountains. My heart longed for the green and the flowers and the trees. I was homesick. I wanted to go home. A voice said to me, "Well, that's easy. If you want to go home, just step off the edge of this steeple." Walking to the edge of the tower, I looked down. Way down I could see tiny people and miniature cars. I said to this unseen voice, "If I step off this steeple, why I'll kill myself." And the voice said, "Take it or leave it. It's the only way."

My attention was drawn by a crowd that had gathered behind me. The people seemed angry, irritated, more like a mob than your typical ladies' mission group. They were discussing me. "What does she think she's doing?" "What's wrong with her?" "Is she crazy?" They began, their voices rising, to beckon me away from the edge, to come back and join them.

As I stood there pondering my choices, the thought of never seeing the trees and the grass and the streams, never seeing home again was so grievous that it outweighed my fear of death. With the turbulence behind me now crescendoing to a scream, I walked to the edge of the tower and stepped off. In that moment a big rope appeared in front of me. Grabbing the rope, I swung far out from the building. Then I realized that if I kept holding that rope, I would soon swing right back to the edge of the building I had just left. I wouldn't be any closer home. Glancing back at the crowd, looking down at the tiny street with the tiny cars, I took a deep breath and let go. Just as I thought I would plummet, another rope appeared. I grabbed it and swung way out again. As it reached its height, another rope appeared, and I grabbed it. Then another and another. Time and time again, trusting that voice, I swung out over the abyss until I finally reached home.

What does this dream have to do with the spirituality of leadership? Everything! Dreams are important because they bring us to the edge of the mystery. They arise from the power of the collective subconscience. They call us to experience something beyond ourselves. I know what the dream means for me: *As I swing out over the rim, as I step beyond the limits, as I grab each newly offered rope, I am a woman who is leading the way home.*

It is hard for me to believe that my leadership is important. It may be hard for any of us to believe that what we are doing as leaders in this time is central to leading people home. We feel we cannot lead. It has been difficult for me to believe that who I am and what I have to offer through my presence are not just peripheral, tangential, unimportant. Excellent leadership, we feel, is for others to give but not for us. The rest of us simply stumble along as best we can. On the contrary, who we are and what we offer are central to fulfilling our leadership task.

What Is This Changing Business, Anyway?

Perhaps you felt, when asked to serve in your present leadership position, the way I felt when called to be a leader. Never in my wildest dreams had I envisioned myself as a leader among leaders. Me tell you how to lead? How to do it, whatever it is? I know people are watching and waiting. They want everything and expect nothing. There are mornings when I awaken and know I have to be "on." I simply want to roll over, pull those nice, warm blankets over my head, snuggle with my cat, and go back to sleep. I don't want to do this anymore! Reach out to change the world? Such unabashed boldness!

The government threatened to cut off Sarah (Sadie) and Elizabeth (Bessie) Delany's government checks unless they could prove they were still alive. While both were over one hundred years old, they certainly were alive, and they proved it in the best-selling book, *Having Our Say*. Born the daughters of the first elected black Episcopal bishop, the Delany sisters were distinguished graduates of Columbia University. Bessie was only the second black woman licensed to practice dentistry in New York. Sadie was the first black person ever to teach domestic science on the high school level in the New York City public schools. Both of these women, although they did not seek it, became leaders for their time.

These two sages looked back over their lives of struggle. For years they worked in their own ways to make a difference for their people and society. Toward the end of their lives, Bessie wrote: "You had to decide: Am I going to change the world, or am I going to change me? Or maybe change the world a little bit, just by changing me? When I was young nothing could hold me back. It took me a hundred years to figure out I can't change the world. I can only change Bessie. And, honey, that ain't easy either." What I have learned is that you don't change the world by rearranging it. Instead, as you first change yourself, you then change the world.

Sarah's and Elizabeth's reflections give credence to our suspicions. We are faced time and again with a reality that in the grand scheme of things there is really very little we can change. At best we can only change ourselves. I love Anthony De Mello's reflections in *The Song of the Bird:*

> I was a revolutionary when I was young and all my prayer to God was, "Lord, give me the energy to change the world."
>
> As I approached middle age and realized that half my life was gone without my changing a single soul, I changed my prayer to, "Lord, give me the grace to change all those who come in contact with me. Just my family and friends, and I shall be satisfied."
>
> Now that I am an old man and my days are numbered, my one prayer is, "Lord, give me the grace to change myself." If I had prayed for this right from the start I should not have wasted my life.

Creative Risks for Leaders

I've been at this life-changing business for a good many years now, and it isn't easy. Indeed, it's proving to be a most formidable task. Perhaps you have experienced the same thing. Can we change the world only as we change ourselves?

• Can you name times when you stood up against the breakers, only to be flung down on the shore wondering if it was worth the price?
• After upheavals and uncertainty, do you seek comfort in routine and unchanging surroundings?
• What creative risks are you failing to take?
• Do you avoid facing conflict and confrontation at any price? When? How does it feel?
• Do you ever shy away from new people and events? Can you describe the opportunities lost?

Susan supervised workers for a boss who was often inconsiderate and hurtful. She could see the repeated patterns. He was condescending, often blaming her and her staff for mistakes that were his own. Her staff members saw how Susan was treated by the "higher up," and they, therefore, showed her little respect or consideration. Nevertheless, when a position in another department, at a better rate of pay and with more responsibility opened, she did not apply but continued to work for the same boss. When she told me about these experiences, I said it seemed that it might be time for a change in jobs. "How can I do that?" she answered me. "I'd be too embarrassed to tell him I was leaving him. Besides, who knows what my next boss will be like? At least here I know what to expect. Besides, I can handle him."

Susan was a leader who allowed her fear to rule her life. For years she submitted to a situation that caused her grief, acquiescing to the boss's authority over her. Her willingness to remain in the situation showed she had little regard for herself. She lost the respect of coworkers. Once in the situation, she felt powerless to change it. To do so would have risked her boss's disapproval, a risk she was unwilling to take. It seemed easier to remain in an unhappy situation than to set out into the unknown. In the end she was unable to lead others in effective ways. She did not value her own worth enough to speak up, so why would others respect her?

There are times when it seems wiser to live in the present circumstances, as agonizing as they are, than to forge ahead into the unknown. In the present we think we know what to expect and can act out our role accordingly. It seems easier to stick with the status quo than to try something new. Yet when we resist change, even change that would be positive, we can become virtually paralyzed by fear of the unknown. Like Susan, we can allow fear to rule our lives.

Effective leaders step beyond fear to the business of change. We are to make this time and place in which we find ourselves the best it can be. We are being called to

17

change ourselves, to move in new ways and directions to bring this world into alignment with what God intends for our lives and the lives of others. Ask yourself:

• Am I continuing to deceive myself by avoiding the confrontations that keep me stuck and unable to move on?
• Am I refusing to face what needs to be changed, stifling my own growth and spiritual development?

As we make choices for change, we are released to live in faithfulness to the person God calls us to be. We allow ourselves to ride the waves, go with the unpredictable surf, and land safely on shore. Life-giving change within ourselves is crucial if we are to make a difference. Change ourselves? Change the world? As leaders it is a calling we dare not fail to answer.

Leadership Arises from Who I Am

The leader part of my being emerges from who I am. It is not something out there, somehow separate from me, filled with doing it right, meeting the deadline, or adjusting to other's expectations. We can easily get trapped into playing a part. Instead, through years of growing and becoming, I have learned that the leader part of me comes from my inner workings. As I serve from within, my service bears fruit that makes a difference.

Annie Dillard, in her wonderful book *Teaching a Stone to Talk,* speaks about spirituality. What she has to say can be applied to the spirituality of leadership:

> In the deeps are the violence and terror of which psychology has warned us. But if you ride these monsters deeper down, if you drop with them farther over the world's rim, you find what our sciences cannot locate or name, the substrate, the ocean or matrix or ether which buoys the rest, which gives goodness its power for good, and evil its power for evil, the unified field: our complex and inexplicable caring for each other, and for our life together here. This is given. It is not learned.

The journey of leadership is one in which we ride the monsters that invade our souls. We make the inner journey and honestly face the mirrors of our innermost parts. We are unwilling to live life in a flat, shadowy malaise; instead, we face our own darkness so that we can find the light of God. Annie Dillard speaks about the darkness that separates us from the divine. When we fail to move down deeper and deal with what sits just over the rim, the monsters only grow larger. They become more powerful, taking on a life of their own. Leaders have a particular responsibility to stay aware of what is happening inside themselves and their consciousness lest, in their leadership, they cause more harm than good.

Leadership of the IN and DOWN

The journey of leadership is not one that moves us upward and outward, as many popular books on leadership tell us. Feminist spirituality writers give us some clues about what attributes of authentic leadership are missing in the workplace. Leadership "in and down" is not simple. It is not a set formula filled with easy answers to difficult questions. Instead, it requires us to think multi-dimensionally. It insists that we look at the paradoxes of life and glory in the mysteries and complexities of leadership.

Each of us can name persons in our institutions, organizations, or committees, including managers and pastors of congregations, who transfer from one place or position to another without dealing with their difficulties. They have an uncanny ability for messing up, moving on and leaving behind a trail of disappointed, disenfranchised followers. Yet, we need to be careful about pointing fingers at others. Remember the childhood saying, "For every finger I point at someone else, there are always three pointing back at me." It is easier and safer to see these "monster" characteristics in others. It is much harder to examine the snafus caused by our own leadership.

When we take positions of leadership, we have no choice but to journey in and down. What I learned from my mentors is that as we make the time to step away from the craziness of our institutions and churches we can then look at our affairs from a sane place. From that vantage point, we can move outward to the concrete realities of our lives.

Now I'll be frank. I've said to God in my own moment of calling, "I don't want to do that! Just let me study technique of management or get a doctor of ministry in 'spiritology' or a Ph.D. in 'leaderology.' " We've all been hurrying as if we were engaged in a race against time. We were in a hurry to get through school, to get married (or unmarried), and to get where we are today. We have been so rushed that we haven't taken the time for ourselves. We've been the dutiful child or compassionate friend or selfless parent or perfect employee. But how often have we been ourselves or tried to find ourselves?

Raised during the Depression era, Pastor John told everyone that nobody ever died of hard work, and he set out to prove it. He routinely put in sixteen-hour days, all in the interest of being the perfect pastor and committed Christian. He rationalized that he had to work that hard. If he didn't, who else would visit all the sick, get the bulletin out, mail the news-letter, listen to the bereaved, and plan the church school curriculum? Then there were the regional church committees to chair and community invoca-tions to deliver. John could do it all! Well, not quite.

Only after John's second heart attack did it begin to dawn on him that his growing compulsiveness about work had grown completely out of bounds. His behavior gave him an inflated estimate of his ability to keep working to the detriment of his body, which was giving out. Inspecting further, he discovered he was also alienated from his feelings toward family and friends. Suddenly awake, he realized that both of his sons were grown and gone. Even the parish-ioners, whom he professed to serve and lead, came second to his need to keep moving and doing. Over-

*run by his compulsion and a slave to work, he no
longer had his own life. He was truly the walking
dead. He began to question if perhaps he did need
to stop and seek spiritual direction. Why was he so
driven, and to what end?*

If we are not going to lead from darkness but light; if we
are not going to project our own sickness and disease on
those we serve; if we are to stay healthy in the midst of
overwhelming responsibility—then we'd better be willing
as leaders to make the journey inward. As we move and
search inward, we will meet the terror and violence that lie
within us. We will project this same terror out upon the
institutions and people we serve, unless we face it, unless
we allow God to transform us at that deep level. It is there
that we can meet the God who is light at the point of our
own darkness.

Five Affirmations for Leadership

As I consider my inward journey, I realize there are
basics that have been helpful to me. There are four ropes
that I grab and swing with so that I lead in ways that are
healthy and whole. These are spiritually affirming voices
that live inside so I can be the leader I am called to be.

Affirmations are tools that I use to swing out further,
saying a bold "Yes! Now!" to the Divine. Affirmations are
powerful, positive statements that declare how we want to
live as leaders who make a difference. When we allow
ourselves to say "Yes!" to the work of the inner spirit, then
we are able to make the changes we need to make.

Through affirmations we establish a dialogue with ourselves and with God. Working with affirmations, we ask,
"What kind of leadership is emerging from within me?" We
search our life-long dreams, our intuitions, and our deepest desires. Through these affirmations we develop a new
attitude that is ready to listen and to act. We open ourselves to new ways for God's purpose to be worked in and
through us.

The following affirmations for leadership are for those who want to replace worn-out tapes of leadership and negative inner dialogue with positive, life-giving images and language. The messages we absorb about ourselves and the conversations between us and the One Divine Spirit—God—are crucial in determining the kind of leaders we are and the ways we lead. These conversations determine our attitude, outlook, behavior, and path.

Are there parts of yourself that you dislike? Are there other parts you would like to enhance or change? In order to do so you need to set aside time each day to form images of yourself behaving as a Spirit-led leader. I call this time "prayer." Others call it meditation or contemplation. Whatever you call it, using affirmations as guides can change old messages and reverse patterns that no longer fit.

I invite you to claim five affirmations for leadership that have been important for me.

Who Am I?

Affirmation: I am a person of
worth and holiness.

D o you know who you are? Is this an affirmation that is firmly planted at the core of your leading? This is a primary issue for all who wish to lead by the Spirit. Who I am does not depend on what I do or my title, function, or position. Who I am does not depend on my power versus your power. Who I am is based in my own power. I am valued simply because I am.

Even for persons who know who they are, this is a time in many workplaces when identities are being sorely tested. With dwindling budgets, merging of departments, downsizing, cutting of staffs, and shifts in power, some of us live in terror of what will happen to us if our institution or role within the institution disappears. Our identities are so tied up in titles and placement, offices we hold and honors bestowed, and, for that matter, simple job security, that we may literally die if our institutional identities are taken away.

Acknowledge Your Worth and Value

Most of us in leadership positions are extroverts. Yes, it is hard to see insecurity in extroverted people. Extroverts often appear able to handle anything that comes their way. Insecurity is masked. When we feel "up against it," doesn't our extroversion, the face we put on for others, cover our insecurity? We find ourselves putting out more and more, trying harder and harder to prove our worth to an external world. Anxiety attacks and nervous stomachs often lie beneath a seemingly placid surface. We pay a high price for our hidden fears and expectations.

We need to pause, go inward, and acknowledge our own worth. We need to find the strength to be who we are instead of who we think we are supposed to be. When we fail to do so, the consequences can be paralyzing for both ourselves and our organization.

We have all lived under the fallout of leaders who are in the grips of this kind of insecurity and unknown identity. In our own most precarious times, some of us have been sucked into its undertow. Many times, people are abusive because, in their depths, they feel worthless; therefore, over and over they try to prove their value with power. As we work with them, we experience the strangling desperation of a leader who makes others "less than" so they can feel "more than." These leaders strip and deprive other people of their identities so that they can enhance their own identities and feel secure.

What Do Spiritually Insecure Leaders Look Like?

We see this demonstrated repeatedly. Bosses require title and surname while secretaries are not given the same respect and are called only by their first names. Physicians and clergy carry their credentials "Doctor" or "Reverend," while patients or clients and parishioners are known with no honor of title, not even Mr., Ms, or Mrs. The bishop is often addressed in a formal manner, while his or her conversation partner is not. The word, spoken or implied, is that "less than" people of organizations are not to create their own space or promote their own portfolio or individual identities. Instead, the "less than's" identity is to be the institution. This institutional culture, created by people in power who are themselves in severe identity crisis, cannot be a spiritually healthy place to work. These leaders work in ways that make institutions malfunction.

Today's reality is that people don't trust systems. People trust people. The flower children of the 1960s and 1970s carried the slogan "Don't trust anyone over thirty." Twenty-five years later, this slogan continues to be lived out in revised ways. These people, now in their forties, don't trust systems of government, corporations, or the organized church. Bureaucracies are suspect, even as these now-grown flower children step into more and more leadership positions. They are no longer willing to meld into impersonal systems and institutional cultures. They want to be valued and treated as persons of worth. Effective leadership, operating from a solid base of Spiritwork, enables each person as well as the team to succeed.

What Do Spiritually Secure Leaders Look Like?

When you are in an organization led by persons who know who they are all the way down inside themselves, who are not fearful of losing their positions or jobs, whose identities do not depend on a role that could be taken from them at any moment, then you are with people who can empower others to be the whole persons they are created to be.

To live in one's own power through God's Spirit means we no longer have to control or manipulate anyone or anything. I am freed from trying to control or to make you into who I think you should be. I no longer have the driving need to make you over into who I need and want you to be. This allows me to accept you for who you are, not expecting you to be someone you are not and cannot be. Now you can work better and more efficiently, free from my overbearing presence. The Spirit frees us to be our complete creative selves and allows others to do the same.

The Scarcity Model

I would like us to look at two models of power—one that is healthy and life-giving and one that is sick and death-dealing. The book *Leadership for Change*, by Bruce Kokopeli and George Lakey, gives important models for the use of power by leaders. The first example is called the "scarcity model." The scarcity model is this: If you have four apples and give away four apples, then you will have no apples. People who believe there is limited power hold on to every last one of their apples. I suspect that these persons' ways of leadership are not ripe for the harvest, but may be rotten to the core.

My boss, Mr. Richards, had a sign on his desk that read, "The buck stops here." However much he dele-gated tasks or appeared to ask others' opinions, I and everyone else knew that the ultimate power rested with him. He liked to be on top of everything, and we all learned to let him know what we were doing before we made a move. It was safer that way. As long as I followed the rules and kept the status quo, I knew I'd be all right and not need to be out job hunting.

Scarcity-model leadership means that the final authority is vested in one person. The boss's sign let everyone know that the real power was held by the person at the top—Mr. Richards. These organizational structures, no matter what the diagram on paper shows, are still the old pyramid style. The preoccupation is control and compliance. The leader controls through threats, which can range from financial and physical intimidation to the elimination of positions. Such a leader prevents other staff from performing leadership functions. With aggressiveness, the scarcity-model leader can face down any challenge to his or her authority.

My boss, Alice Stephens, always reminds me of a female Mr. Anderson in "Father's Knows Best." I hate to be talking about her like this. She is a nice, likable woman, good at solving problems. But, even though I'm her assistant, she's slow to share her skills with me, and I can tell by her manner that she doesn't think I, or anyone, can do things as well as she can. She is a very nurturing person and really cares. In fact, she is constantly doing things for other people. She likes to be helpful. When something needs doing, she sees that it gets done, even if it means at her own expense. We all feel indebted. Not only is she our leader, but also she shows such caring and self-sacrifice! A lot of nights after the rest of us go home, Dr. Stephens stays and keeps on working. She really takes on responsibility, especially in times of crisis. I wouldn't want to do what she does. I try to do my part, and I certainly don't want to disappoint her.

The tension inside this "mother knows best" style of leadership is enormous. It is difficult to play the "nice gal or guy" and maintain power, especially if one is to discipline, hire, and fire. Needless to say, there is a lot of messiness in personnel matters. How can she call someone to accountability or even fire anyone with out appearing "un-nice"?

Another source of tension in this kind of leadership is in how this leader gets his or her own personal needs met. Remember, this indirect control can only be maintained through a "doing for others" posture. It is difficult to maintain power through overextending yourself for others and still care for your own needs. After a short time, this leader becomes spiritually bankrupt, and everyone else pays.

Dr. Stephens came by my desk yesterday. I could sense that she was feeling lonely. It turns out that her executives went over her head to ask for changes in the department. "How can they do this to me, after all I've done for them?" she asked me. How could I explain it to her? We feel so ambivalent. I kept my mouth shut. I know she feels we are all ungrateful, and in one sense she's right. We are grateful in one sense, but we also feel resentful of how we have to depend on her for so much. Maybe it's the company that's calling the shots, like she says, but we feel that she could allow us to have some rights and power too.

It is clear that power and control are firmly in the leader's grasp. The ambivalence and unfocused anger of her colleagues will either lead the leader to a quiet ineffi-ciency that will drive the leader to distraction or the followers to an angry, open revolt. The leader cares, but group members and workers find it very hard to make needed changes without rebelling against her.

People are abusive in power when they feel powerless. Some leaders who appear to claim a great deal of power feel powerless. They live in the belief that there is only so much power to go around. Power is limited, and if they give away their power, they will have none.

The Multiplication Model

In truth, power is limitless. There is power for everyone. As we share our resources, information, and space, other individuals will claim their own power. This does not take away from our own power, but enhances the total commu-nity. It is when we give away that we receive. This second model is called the "multiplication model" of power. If you have good news and give it to four people, and they give it to four people and they continue to share, then the good

28

news is multiplied and limitless. The good news here is one of shared power. I would not have written this book if someone had not taken the risk of operating out of a shared power model of leadership. In a warm, affirming manner, these spiritual, professional mentors taught me some very important and tangible understandings about leadership. Let's examine the roles and functions of leaders who work from the multiplication model of leadership.

First, leadership is a function. It is not a place of power vested in one person. There is not one person in a group who is the only one who leads. Instead, if the person "in charge" is a good leader, she or he will facilitate. Allow each member of the group to assume leadership sometime during the meeting or work process. There is an important difference between the "role" of leadership and the "functions" of leadership.

Here is an example so that you may better understand the differences between the role and functions of leadership. As the designated leader, I am given the authority to be in charge and help the group meet its goal (the role), but each member of the group exerts leadership and performs leadership functions at some time (the function). Functions of leadership might include giving support and encouraging members, creating fun to relieve tension in the group, serving as the process observer, or being the summarizing person who pulls together related ideas and summarizes them for the group.

These functions and many others we could name are all important in leading. It would be next to impossible to expect one person to perform all of these functions for the entire group. That is why it is important for the designated leader to give permission and, even at times, assign different functions to individuals. I am sure you have seen these functions happen naturally within groups you've worked with. At other times, the leader must be more intentional and name the expectation to group members for this to happen.

Jill Wilson is a truly inspirational leader. I love working with her. When she is leading a meeting, I know I'll leave feeling that I haven't wasted my time and that we've all really accomplished something! I remember once when the group came to an impasse. We just couldn't come to an agreement so that we could proceed. Jill never seemed shaken. She simply restated our goals and held up to us again the ultimate vision of the group. This put us in an optimistic framework so we could try again.

We recognize that she's the leader, and we respect her for the role she plays in helping us process. But what she does is turn the group not to her own agenda, but toward us so we can see the vision and renew our resolve to work toward its completion. She doesn't have to be the center of the conversation or force things to come out her way. I always leave the meetings with clarity, knowing I can do my part!

Second, good leaders demystify the way things work. Others see what is happening. They share all information needed and teach everyone the skills of group process so that the group can function without anyone monopolizing, including you! With each person learning to experience his or her own power, each feels an equal stake in achieving the goals and maintaining group spirit.

I couldn't have done it without his help. George Stark was retiring and encouraged me to apply for his position. When it was offered, I knew I was in over my head, but I accepted because George said he'd not leave me stranded. In fact, it was arranged so he could stay and work with me to get me on board. There was so much to learn. A class on my new computer system got me up and running. We went through the books and files step be step so I would understand the total picture. Most important, he shared with me the intricacies of the job and the personalities involved. This kept me from being sabotaged or unwittingly stepping into something I wasn't prepared for. He sure saved me a lot of grief!

I learned a lot watching him interact with his colleagues. He, through his modeling and gentle mentoring, showed me that it isn't hard to learn group process. Now I know how to keep persons from monopolizing, how to put the members of the group in charge and keep things in the open by sharing the process as well as conclusions with others. That means I, as the leader, don't make pronouncements but instead tell how I reached my decision.

Third, the spiritual well-being of group members is just as important as getting the job done. The group's functioning depends on the care of its members as does any task undertaken. Build confidence in each person. That is just as important as learning new skills, for people must have confidence in themselves or the skills go unused.

I've been part of the office staff, working as Natalie's supervisor for five years. I've grown to appreciate her leadership and have learned how to hone my own skills. Overseeing the work of nine other people is hard work. I've had to unlearn some old leadership patterns I learned in the past. I have good people working with me. I give support to the individuals in my department, help them through good feedback, and trust them to make their own decisions. I've learned through my own experience that people grow best in an atmosphere of warm affirmation.

Working Together for Creative Solutions

One rainy night my husband, seven-year-old son, Stephen, and I were playing Scrabble. We selected the required seven lettered tiles, hiding them from one another, and the game began. We were prepared to pit our word abilities against one another until "the best one won." Of course, Dale and I played the part of the good parents. With each play, one of us leaned over to help our second grader. In this way he could feel he had a part in the game, even if the real contest was between his dad and me.

Then Stephen, growing impatient with our help, began to tell us how we might play the game differently. What if we worked together to use every word? We could probably even use those hard-to-place X's and Z's, he explained. We laughed together at the novelty of the plan. Working together with a common goal made the game easier instead of harder. Creative solutions appeared from the shared mind between us. Stephen no longer felt patronized but an integral part of the full plan. Besides, we had more fun working together!

The good news is that the multiplying example of power is enriching and whole, joyous and freeing. Because I am a person of worth and holiness and know who I am, the Spirit frees me to live out my leadership in power-filled ways. This opens up the possibility of sharing with others so that they, too, can claim their power.

Leading with Love

Affirmation: I am a lover who lives out my love in mutuality, connectedness, and community.

As a leader, who am I at my deepest part? Who am I as one created by God? Because God is one who comes to us in the depths, we are bound to God first and foremost. Because God has been with me since the moment of birth, because God has carried my struggles and is and was there in my pain and hurt and dysfunction, because God has not abandoned me but surrounded me with goodness and mercy and love, I am bound to God first and forever. God is love. Love is my own deepest nature and desire. As a leader, I lead out of God's nature of love. I am a natural lover.

Do you work with persons who operate out of a different view of life? Can you spot persons who believe that their colleagues are out only for what they can personally gain for themselves? Can you recognize those who believe they are in competition against you? I would like to assert that these persons work out of something other than love as their basic nature. They work under the sad presumption that "first and foremost, all people are sinners." They watch coworkers and colleagues, suspecting them of ulterior motives that will, in the end, heighten the other person's standing in the company and diminish their own. They diligently watch for the stab in the back or the undermining of authority. The scarcity-power model is in full operation, "There is only so much power to go around, and I'm going to make sure I have mine!"

I shudder when I hear and see leaders working from this premise. To look through the tainted lens of "sinner" at all one's relationships is to believe people are basically filled with, as one biblical writer stated in his letter to a quarrelsome community, "selfish ambition and conceit." It is to propagate the belief that we are in competition with one another and if we don't compete we lose. How grievous! When we talk and act in this way, when we live in these beliefs, we create a self-fulfilling prophecy. We create a competition that divides and separates us from each other. In the movie *It's a Wonderful Life*, starring Jimmy Stewart and Donna Reed, the bank became insolvent only because people panicked and believed it was. Could it be that the Spirit is telling us that the world is competitive only because we have chosen not to live otherwise?

Give the Reasonable Doubt of Goodness

As a person who strives to operate out of goodness and love, I make the choice to err on the side of love and grace. That is, when examining another persons actions, I'd rather give him or her a reasonable doubt of goodness than automatically suspect him or her of acting out of selfishness, greed, or vindictiveness aimed at me. It is my belief that people are not essentially evil. Individuals may simply be thoughtless. People don't take the time to think through all the implications of their actions. They don't take the time to ask, "Who else will be affected by what I do?" They don't take the initiative to work though relational matters before acting in ways that will affect others' lives. It takes more energy to decide and do the loving and gracious thing.

34

We have to steadfastly work toward that goal. When it seems that those you work with are purposely sabotaging your efforts or may not be appreciative of your best efforts, do you feel paranoid? As one colleague expressed tongue-in-cheek, "I wouldn't be so paranoid if everyone wasn't against me!"

Do you think at times that people operate out of an intent to harm you? Sometimes it has felt that way to me. Yet, after examining all the facts (except for a very few cases), I don't think so. We give people too much credit! These persons are not purposely sabotaging our efforts; instead, they are unthinking. Out of their own ignorance of the situation, they unknowingly make decisions that are not in others' best interest. They simply hold others in "unregard" and don't think of others before they move to action.

It takes forethought and planning to viciously scale an attack against another. Most people, in the rush of the day, simply don't put that much energy into such endeavors. What we name as espionage is more likely neglectful or unthinking persons stuck in the rut of a system that does not take into consideration caring for individual needs. This is where sin comes in. That's right. I used that old-fashioned word *sin.* Whatever the reason for not "loving our neighbor as ourselves" or not "doing unto others as we would have them do unto us," their actions cannot be excused. It is still sin!

Sin is the wrong that we do when we act in unloving ways toward another person. It is sin that separates, hurts, puts down, and does not affirm other people as valuable children of God. It is sin when we build unloving barriers between us and our creator and other people.

———————

Supervisor Judy's secretarial staff had put in long, hard hours preparing for the big convention. When the week finally arrived, they added more time in directing the registration, caring for technical details, and doing the nitty-gritty floor work of each day's business. The Monday following the event, the

*department director invited members of the staff,
both secretarial and professional, to share around
the table the one thing they appreciated about their
work at the convention. Each staff member shared a
story highlighting new learnings and expressing appreciation of others who had helped make the time
enjoyable. When Judy's turn to praise the secretaries in front of the entire staff came, she glanced up
from her note taking and said, "We survived," smiled,
and returned to her note pad.*

Staff members slumped; their faces fell as their enthusiasm died. Judy's betrayal let them down. How sad for all
of them. Perhaps it is by default that we don't operate out
of love more often. Love and sin are both at work in us. A
person makes an intentional choice to operate in loving
ways. Each day, each hour, and each moment we con-
sciously decide to turn from sin and work in the reality of
love. It isn't easy. In fact, it's very hard!

Original Goodness

We are part of God's original goodness. I believe that it
was God's original intention in forming the universe and
every living thing that all creation would reflect the goodness of God's self. What God inspired was good. The
opposite of possessing the goodness of God is something
we were taught to call "original sin." Eknath Easwaran, in
his book *Original Goodness,* is inclined toward a new
understanding of human nature. When all hostility, all
resentment, all greed and fear and insecurity are erased
from your minds, the state that remains is pure joy. When
we become established in that state, we live in joy always.

There, the mystics of all religions agree, we uncover our
original goodness. We don't have to buy it; we don't have
to create it; we don't have to pour it in; we don't even have
to be worthy of it. This native goodness is the essential core
of human nature. The purpose of all valid spiritual disci-
plines, whatever the religion from which they spring, is to

36

enable us to return to this native state of being—not after death but here and now, in unbroken awareness of the divinity within us and through creation. Theologians may quarrel, but the mystics of the world speak the same language, and the practices they follow lead to the same goal.

There seems to be a distortion in what some call original sin or fall/redemption theology. This theology ignores the fact that we are created in the image of a God of love. My children are created in God's image. As a mother, holding them in my arms in their first moments of life, I knew they were not enemies of the world. They were not sinful, in the classic use of the word, but children of God, children of love. They would become sinners only as they interacted with the world and failed to take responsibility for their own actions.

Love Means Taking Responsibility

Schindler's List retells the poignant story of the Holocaust in which millions of Jews were exterminated. Their lives were snuffed out as insignificant. As a graduate student I visited the Buchenwald concentration camp where millions of people were tortured, gassed, beaten, hanged, and shot. Walking past the incinerators, I was unable to breathe, not wanting to believe what had happened there. I recalled my visit, as I watched the anguished, tangled story of distrust, hate, and fear unfold on the movie screen. Many were "just taking orders," "following procedures"—"I just work here, lady." Only a very few took responsibility. My popcorn sat untouched. I thought I would vomit. In shock, I watched the ending credits roll by. Leaving the theater, I went to wash my face and gather myself together. Never before had I witnessed human brutality so vividly.

I had to ask again, Is there an original sin? What is the basic nature of our being? Is it love or is it truly sin? And if it is love, what has pulled or driven us into the state in which we now live? How have we gone so far astray? Sin is missing the mark of what God intended. Sin happens as we interact with the world. It is when we refuse responsibility.

If there is a lesson in the story of Adam and Eve, it is this: When God asked Adam why he had eaten the fruit, Adam pointed to the woman and said, in essence, "She made me do it." When the woman was asked why she ate the fruit, she pointed to the snake and said, "The snake made me do it." Neither Adam nor Eve took responsibility. Perhaps, part of the understanding of original sin can be unearthed in our not living responsibly. Does original sin become our excuse for not living responsibly and continuing to live in disastrous ways?

God's Divine Spark Is at the Center

As I sat for the next two days, sorting out *Schindler's List*, I realized that if there was a commonality on both sides, it seemed to be fear. The Nazis feared that if they didn't have all the power, then it wasn't enough to live and not fear for their own lives. They operated out of a scarcity model of power with devastating results. Each person in the drama had someone above him or her with more power who could exterminate them. This fear (aside from exceptional cases), made everyone distrust everyone else and act out of the need for self-preservation. The fear kept their eyes closed to seeing God's divine spark in other people and honoring that same spirit in each person they met.

For love to be at the center of our lives together, we remember and know that God is in everyone. There is a divine spark at the center of each person's being. As we unite with the holy, purest love, we are enabled to love others. The task of loving others is achievable only as we join ourselves in God's love. I am not more special or of less value than you. I am not vastly different or more or less perfect than you. It is when we make the faulty assumption that somehow we are better and of higher status or worth less than others and of lower status in the Creator's eyes that sin gathers momentum. It is when we

effect that telling someone to "have a nice day" has in caring for depression. Many of us have lived too long in numbness, denial, and craziness.

What does it mean to make choices that are reoriented and rooted in this reality of love?

• *It means making the choice to fast, to facilitate prayer, meditation, and direction.*

Do you give yourself permission to have time alone? Do you take time, even fifteen minutes apart, and make the choice to fast? I'm not talking about fasting as in giving up food. Fasting is a proven ancient practice that refreshes the soul. Instead of forgoing food, think of fasting as stepping away from those things that overwhelm you, those things that pollute your day. Think of fasting from things that separate you from yourself, from God, and from other people. Plan to take a conscience break. You might fast from the television or radio, news reports or the telephone. I find it especially important, from time to time, to fast from people. I need time alone, so I step away from even those persons closest to me if I am to continue to love them. In this time of fasting, live in the spaciousness of the moment. Try fasting, and you'll be surprised at what fills the space.

• *It means not growing weary in continually tearing down the walls I build around my heart.*

Are you hurt by people time and again? Are you sometimes tempted to make a hard and fast rule not only to shut out individuals but also to completely shut down on everyone and everything? The outcome of this wall building can be numbness. Just for today, choose your battles carefully. You cannot fight all the battles that need to be fought. There are just too many. Choose those that are truly worthy of your efforts and where you feel you can make a difference. Make a prayerful note to hand the rest over to God.

• It means journeying through my inner pain, despair, and loneliness.

Are you carrying old baggage from the past as you walk into the future? Do you feel as if you are in a rut, dragging through your days with clouded eyes? Are you in touch with your feelings? If you feel disconnected, then there may be hard work to be done. Just for today, seek out a discerning friend, helpful counselor, or spiritual mentor who can assist you to see your past in ways that will help you live today in all its fullness.

• It means reconciling within myself those who have not loved me as I've needed.

Were your earlier years less than perfect? Most were. We were raised by adults who had their own problems. Did you experience disappointment as you entered adulthood? Let's face it, this grown up stuff wasn't what was advertised! The world did not deliver what we thought it promised. Whatever love you did or didn't receive as a child, perhaps it is never enough to prepare you for such a hard world. Most of us have been disappointed in love. In any case, you need to come to grips with what could have been better or worse in your relationships. Then use these lessons to better understand and work within your present relationships to make them the best they can be.

• It means taking responsibility for my part in life.

Do you feel responsible for all the people or situations around you? Do you feel like it's up to you to always remember everyone's birthday, make the coffee, or break the silence at meetings? You are not "on duty" twenty-four hours a day. It is not your responsibility to make sure that everyone is comfortable and that every detail is cared for. It's too exhausting, so, beginning today, refuse to live this way. Do what you can do in a sensible fashion and at a reasonable pace. Starting now, allow others to take responsibility.

Of course, there are parts of life we can't control—the death of a loved one, the alcohol addiction of a family member, the choices other people make. But there are responsibilities that are ours. How you act in different situations is your choice. Your choices and your actions can make a difference. You take responsibility for these decisions.

• *It means reclaiming my place with my lover God.*

Do you take time to be with God? Loving, intimate relationships require time together. You might begin to carry a small book of short meditations, affirmations, or pocket scriptures to reflect on short passages. Beware of "feel good" meditations and self-absorbed, "cutsey" stories. Choose reading that beckons you to go where you have never been. Whatever you choose, make sure it is based on and drawn from the "timeless"—the psalms, the Gospels, and other inspired texts.

Take time to read and reflect on some holy words each day. Go to a place alone, either physically or mentally, and talk out loud or write your thoughts on paper. These ways of prayer and meditation will help give form to your feelings and thoughts, reminding you that you're not crazy! Taking time out for God in worship, praise, and song, alone and in community, is important to your relationship with God.

Prayer: Reconnecting with Our Lover

An ancient oral-tradition story was shared with me. Although its origin is unknown, its truths are enduring. A great leader and spiritual mentor sojourned in the land, teaching followers the fundamentals of spirit-filled leadership. One student, especially eager to learn the ways of the Spirit, approached the mentor following the day's lesson. The student asked his mentor if she might instruct him further in the ways of prayer, reflection, and meditation. The great leader smiled and nodded. When they met, the student, tablet in hand, was eager to learn the techniques and variations of prayer.

Lowering herself to her knees, all the mentor said was, "You wish to learn about prayer? Let's pray." To the student's amazement, the spiritual leader said not another word to him, but proceeded to pray through the night and far into the wee hours of the morning. Unsuccessfully fighting off sleep, the student wove in and out of wakefulness, sleeping more than praying. In the morning, the student awoke and found himself lying on the floor and his mentor missing.

The spiritual mentor demonstrated that prayer is one Spiritwork that leaders must go ahead and do, knowing they will never fully understand the mystery. In Spiritwork, we need prayer. There are no short cuts.

Sometimes the pressures of leadership overwhelm you.

• Do you ever become so busy rushing from one task to another or one place to another that you lose your inner vision?
• Does your mind race?
• Do the answers you seek recede further into the background with each new item that captures your attention?

During these times, stop and ask what is happening. Quiet yourself long enough to hear wisdom's message. In quieting yourself before God, you will find the answer is there as you are ready to listen.

Created by God to Be Lovers

If we can be reoriented and rooted in these new ways of being, we will, for the first time, live in the reality of who we are and were created to be: lovers. To think of ourselves as lovers in this context may be foreign to us. We are uncomfortable with the image of God or ourselves as lovers because of the way the term is currently used to suggest sexual images. But isn't it what we are really all about? The Hebrew Scriptures read, "You shall love the Lord your

God with all your heart, and with all your soul, and with all your might" and "You shall love your neighbor as yourself."

Yes. I still believe, as one created of the divine, that love is the first and final word. Love is my own deepest nature and desire.

Love is the deeper dimension that lies below the deception. In the deepest, innermost part of my being, who I am is not sin but love. I am not happy except when I am loving. I am at peace only when I am loving others in connection and intimacy. Peace makers love greatly and are great lovers. My deepest longing is to be with God, the supreme lover. To be joined with God is to be one with love. Rested and warm in this order, I can dare to swing out, reaching for the next rope knowing I am both loved and loving. To follow the sacred teachings, to love God and our neighbors as ourselves, we must first be lovers.

Who's in Charge Here, Anyway?

Affirmation: I am empowered to live
God's will as I co-create with others.

A mysterious disease runs through the leaders of our institutions, organizations, businesses, and even religious communities. Someone named it. It's labeled *functional atheism*. It's a virus easily caught. Believe me, I know. Oh, some of us would be the last people who would claim to be atheists, but actions speak louder than words. Let's check our pulse to see if we're susceptible. Have you ever caught the germ that says, "If you want something done, you'd better do it yourself"? Does your behavior say, "If anything is going to happen here, I must be the one to make it happen"? If you answered yes to either of these two questions, then you may be revealing your own functional atheism. There are visible symptoms of this disease, too. Functional atheism can be seen in the fact that most groups can sit still for only fifteen seconds of silence. Time the silences in worship services or when someone calls for a period of silence in memory of a loved one. Not many seconds, much less minutes, are actually given for silent prayer or reflection. Have you ever felt the compelling urge to speak, believing that "if I'm not speaking then nothing is happening"? Ultimate responsibility rests with me: "I am God."

Consuela was the best volunteer! Everyone in the community knew that if you needed a person who could take a project to completion, Consuela was that person. When a committee or task group was floundering, Consuela could be counted on to jump in, complete everyone's task, and bring the event off in good form to the applause of everyone. Consuela asked her husband, when he asked if she was going to a committee meeting yet another night, "If I don't do this, who will?" Indeed, Consuela had once again set herself up as the only one who had all the information needed to pull off the latest endeavor. She gained a sense of power and influence she didn't have elsewhere. She was irreplaceable.

After a particularly long, hard fund drive for the new library, Consuela suddenly took ill, collapsing the day after its opening. Her doctor put her in the hospital a few days. Diagnosis: exhaustion.

Exhibiting symptoms of stress and burnout, Consuela's disease is not only acute but chronic and progressive as well. Taking the half measures by treating the symptoms will not help Consuela's underlying spiritual disease. What are the thought patterns of those who acquire this unhealthy type of atheistic behavior? Consuela was not co-creating. She was attempting to do it all herself, to prove her value to herself and to others. Remember the scarcity model of power? We know the pattern well: The more power we have, the more power we have to lose. The more power we have to lose, the more entrenched we become. The more entrenched we become, the more we grasp for certainty. And in the end, we do not lovingly lead by faith. We don't even love ourselves.

As the person in charge and ultimately responsible, Consuela was exhilarated by the pressures of deadlines. At the same time, she worked compulsively to exceed everyone's expectations, fearful that others would think less of her if she didn't consistently achieve high results. Her underlying fear, unacknowledged even to herself, was that if she was not perfect, everyone would know what she knew. They would see what an utter failure she really was. Since her whole being rested on proving her worth over and over, to herself as well as to others, Consuela could not delegate tasks to others, fearing that they would fail to meet her high standard of perfection. They would not accomplish the task in the way that she knew was "the way." Persons with different ideas and concepts could not be trusted. In Consuela's eyes, the assignment would not be done as correctly and other persons' imperfection would reflect on her and spell ultimate failure.

I don't mean to imply that leaders should embrace every new idea that comes through the door. Neither can nor should every new concept be automatically assimilated. There is a piece of me that wants God to be the same yesterday, today, and tomorrow. We like the control that validates our personal worth to the detriment of others. We fear the different. We are fearful people. The media exploit our fears by selling the bizarre. Geraldo, Donahue, and Oprah dispense attention-grabbing one-liners to sell the outrageous and the violent. Television evangelists enjoy drawing graphic pictures detailing the fires of hell and torment following the rapture. Even weather forecasters get into the act, exploiting the audience's excitability, predicting "warnings" and "watches." We need to be careful lest we're taken in by these fear/excitement centered ways of seeing life.

To Live Faithfully: Fully in Faith

Thank goodness God is not so easily boxed in by our fear. God calls us to live not by fear, but by faith. To live faithfully—that is, fully in faith—we live each day, one day at a time. We live the best way we know how for the person we are in each moment. To live by faith, to live fearlessly, we begin with today. You don't live day after day fearful, fearful, fearful and then suddenly awake one morning and say, "I think I'll live fearlessly today." It doesn't work that way. Instead, we awaken each morning to live courageously.

This is easier said than done! How do we begin right now to live our lives with courage? Having courage does not mean that you are without fear. It means that you are willing to act in spite of it. We all have fear, but we don't have to be our fear. Many of us live days with what I call the "pit in the stomach" feeling. Mixed into the depths of the pit are stress, anxiety, and fear, all unfocused. Three keys to being courageous and working past and in spite of the pit are to gain insight, to learn persistence, and to practice, practice, practice.

Insight, Perseverance, and Practice

Insight, perseverance, and practice are the main ingredients necessary to live courageously. To have insight, you must first separate those problems you can do something about from those over which you have no control. Then demonstrate, at least to yourself, that you have the capacity to influence something. Many of us have lived for years with a lack of insight, to our own detriment and to the loss of those we are called to lead.

As soon as my colleague Kenyata said "Hello," I knew he was upset. "Life is so unfair!" were his first words. Kenyata was twenty-six and worked for a company that advertised for the computer industry. He dreamed of becoming an executive. When I inquired why he was upset, he spoke about his inept boss, his less-than-helpful coworkers, the inefficiency of the computer system, and the lack of helpful support staff. In rising agitation, he told of his plan, developed more than four months earlier, to overhaul the management of the office. It would give greater efficiency in day-to-day operations and better service to the customers.

"So what's the problem?" I asked.

The problem, he moaned, was that a colleague had just submitted a similar proposal, polishing it first with his associates before taking it to the boss. It had been approved for immediate implementation. His colleague was now receiving a promotion into a managerial position. "The promotion should have been mine," he lamented. "He just beat me to it!"

When I questioned Kenyata if the colleague had stolen his idea, he said, "No, I never shared the idea with anyone, but it was my idea! Life is so unjust!"

"Kenyata," I said, "anyone can have an idea. What makes the idea work is when someone does something with it. Look at what your colleague did. He had a good idea, refined it with peers, and risked presenting it for possible implementation. That's what made the difference."

What puzzled me was why Kenyata had not shared his insight with anyone. Later he explained that he had felt that if his idea was so good surely someone else would have thought of it before he did. Many live with a little voice inside their heads that says, "If the idea occurred to me—how good can it be?"

Do you ever feel that you'll not be taken seriously so you don't expect to be listened to? Do you dismiss your own ideas as unimportant and then become angry when others don't value you more than you value yourself? In reality, you don't listen to yourself or take yourself seriously.

Having insight is important. But just as strategic is trusting your ability to step out with your ideas. Take them seriously and persevere; nurture and promote them. Face the fears holding you back. Do you fear failure? Do you take yourself seriously? If you don't, why would anyone else? Remember that not every idea will always be implemented. Everyone endures times of disappointment and trial. The ability to persevere in spite of the struggle is what makes the difference.

And practice, practice, practice. This means putting your insights and ideas into action time and again. Each time you step out to try something new, you will grow more competent and more confident! Once you have experienced putting a new idea into practice, you will be led to a second and a third success, creating a domino effect. Slowly, bit by bit, the "pit in the stomach" feeling will disappear. With your new view of yourself as a leader there is an expanded sense of living and a new feeling of authenticity.

We have to live bravely today in the faith that God acts in new ways for new situations. That's part of the plan—to live life as the world can be right now. If we want the new reality right now, we must live it right now! That's how it works. If we really, deeply, profoundly believe in the power of the good news of a new vision, we can do it. But as long as we cherish the vision of how things should be for tomorrow, but not today, then we won't see it happen today. When we collectively believe more in the power of love than in the power of fear, then change can happen.

Driven or Called?

The disease that we've labeled functional atheism is a form of drivenness. Driven people are competitive, striving, and struggling. They lack a sense of balance and live in the waves of extremes. They see the world and their choices in it as all or nothing. In their unhealthy ways, they are either overindulgent or neglectful; in relationships, clingy or unattached; in friendships, overbearing or withdrawn.

Some of us work more out of our drivenness than out of our "calledness." Do you sometimes:

• work more out of what others are driving you to be, rather than what your own inner spirit dictates?
• look at other people's responses to decide how to act?

• allow the source of your approval to reside in other people?
• find yourself "auditioning" for others, pretending to be someone you're not, hoping they will affirm your worth?
• hear and use other people's negative opinions as ammunition against your own sense of self-worth?
• maintain relationships that destroy you and cannot fulfill your deep spiritual needs?

Functional atheism creates dysfunctional behavior on every level of our lives. Ask those closest to you, spouses and colleagues. They will tell you the results of such "stinking thinking." It leads to stress and strain, burnout, workaholic behavior, mixed-up priorities, and, ultimately, broken relationships.

Called to Leadership, Not Ownership

Remember King Saul from Sunday school days? Saul was the first in a succession of kings anointed by God to lead the Israelite people. In his best days, Saul was a good king, a wise man. "God gave him another heart" and "the spirit of God possessed him."

Saul was the chosen leader for God's purpose in that time and place. The Bible tells how King Saul, many years later, held on to his power when it was clear that God wanted the young shepherd boy David to take the reins. Saul held on, protected, gathered, and struggled against God's will. He plotted and schemed to block David's path. In the end, Saul, a pathetic figure, destroyed himself. Sadly, he is remembered more for his avenging spirit than for his years of faithful leadership. Saul considered his call to leadership as ownership—something we never do. A hard lesson.

Prizes Worth Winning: The Story of Neville

What prizes in life are worth winning? That is a daunting question. Some of us rush through life, pursuing one thing and then another, fearful that in the end we will find that the only prize worth winning was the prize we managed to lose. We can spend our whole lives building the biggest companies, collecting the nicest clothes, the smartest cars, or the most notorious names in history and still lose our own souls. We can make sure everyone likes us, that we always win arguments and even appear perfect to everyone around us and still lose our souls. I think you get the point.

Author Susan Howatch, in her novel *Ultimate Prizes*, draws from the writings and biographies of past deans and bishops of the Church of England. Howatch weaves a fascinating web. She carefully reconstructs a hierarchical system in which esteemed positions are dangled ever so seductively in front of ambitious suitors. This is the way the church, not so subtly, controls its ranks. I've found her characters uncomfortably true to life. In fact, they are right on target.

Neville Aysgarth, the main character in this novel, is depicted as standing "politically correct" even when his conscience tells him to take the prophetic stance. You see, as a young child he learned his lessons well from his Uncle Willoughby, who taught him to "get on" and "travel far" in his chosen profession. Neville notes in his journal, "Even during the most difficult moments of my childhood I had always been convinced that God was on my side, rewarding all my hard work and good behavior with well deserved prizes."

Desperately groping for the prizes, Neville, the success-ful church bureaucrat, begins a desperate binge of self-sabotage. He dallies in a sexual affair. Infidelity undermines all he has worked for. When his spiritual mentor, his pastor, and his wife each call him to his true self, he is unable to answer. He is unsure now of who his authentic self is. For too long Neville has told himself half-truths. He has lived the rationalizations and role so perfectly that he can no longer see the reality.

When the "Ah-ha!" moment finally comes, following a series of events spelling professional suicide, Neville pain-fully reflects:

But now God was in his heaven, I was in hell and there was no at-one-ment, no sign of Christ. I was cut off from my sources of spiritual strength, absolutely alone. My instinctive reaction, as always, was to put everything right by chasing the next prize, but the only prize in sight was the prize I had won, the prize which was now poised to destroy me, and I did not see how I could survive.

The turning point for Neville comes when he meets with Darrow, his spiritual adviser.

Darrow discovers that Neville has turned everything in his life—his wife, Dido, his children, and even his calling to serve God—into a prize. But why? Darrow resumes the conversation, leading Neville through his own warped thought process.

"And how long have you been chasing the prizes?"
"Oh, forever. It's the way to get on, isn't it? It's the way to stay out of the pit."
"What pit?"
"The failure pit. The one where the coffin is."
"Failure equals death? Winning the prize equals life?"
"I've won everything I've ever wanted—but I've lost all the way along the line."

If we, like Neville, would stop and ask God what we're doing, we would realize that we need a new perspective. We need to see the bigger picture—that each day of our lives has consequences. We would remember that in the grand scheme of things we are not called to the prizes. We are called to lead only for a time. We die to the "ultimate prizes" if we are to truly live.

Ten Leadership Tasks

Leaders who live in God's will, who dare to take the inner journey, learn that not only can others do what needs to be done, but also (surprise! surprise!) that some can do it much better. Spiritual leadership is not an "all knowing" or "Father Knows Best" power vested in one person. In truth, leadership consists of a series of functions that can be shared among many members of the group. This "shifting leadership" does not expect one leader to perform all the functions and roles. All members can exercise leadership within the group. There are certain tasks of leadership that should be accomplished if a group is to reach goals and function in healthy ways. Ask yourself if you are using and teaching the following techniques for effective goal achievement:

• *Propose objectives* and help set goals, delegate tasks, and initiate actions.
• *Offer information* and facts, give opinions, ideas, and suggestions.
• *Ask for information* and facts.
• *Give direction* and help the group develop plans and proceed with a focus.
• *Harmonize for unity;* coordinate the group so it can function smoothly.
• *Track relationship* and the coordination of activities so nothing falls through the cracks.
• *Diagnose the difficulties* and obstacles that block the group from achieving its goal.
• *Check reality* to examine the workability and practicality of ideas.
• *Suggest alternative solutions* and remind members of history and experiences.
• *Summarize major points* and pull together related ideas and suggestions.

Along with the tasks for goal achievement, leaders also take on roles for the well-being of themselves as well as of group members. These leadership roles, centered in relationships, are just as important as any task accomplished or goal achieved. Leaders encourage the group in difficult times and inspire them to be their best creative selves. Leaders hold up the ultimate vision and place the current situation in an optimistic framework. Encouraging warm support within the group and strengthening connections between individuals is central to leadership. Do a quick self-inventory to discover your current strengths and where you and those you work with need improvement.

Nine Leadership Roles for Well-Being

• *Communicate clearly* and accurately for understanding of all members.
• *Observe the group process*; provide feedback and evaluation for improvement.
• *Listen actively*, accepting input with thoughtful consideration; elicit feelings from members.
• *Track emotions*; help members to name as well as to share their feelings.
• *Promote the resolve* of interpersonal conflicts with open, disciplined discussion.
• *Encourage the group's standards*, norms, and direction; keep the group focused.
• *Create safe space* for ideas to surface and be expressed.
• *Build trust* and be trust worthy.
• *Value the contribution* each person brings; express appreciation openly and often.

Leaders become empowered when they share the load with others. We may even feel free to lay down a few crosses. What makes us think that we've been appointed the saviors of the corporation or the church or the health-care system or whatever our institution is? Other peoples' crosses are other peoples' crosses. They aren't ours. They are for them to bear, not us. We have our own. To assume the weight of the world is to play God. I don't mean to excuse us from the supreme command to work for right-eousness and to be our sisters' or brothers' keepers. We cannot sit back and be inactive and expect things to turn out right. We cannot simply wait and hope that what is wrong will go away. Instead, we give voice and heart to make changes. We have the wonderful opportunity and responsibility to participate in the bigger picture.

In shared leadership, we ask the question together, "What is it that we want to create?" What is the interconnected answer? This cannot be some hierarchical mandate handed down from on high. It cannot be the words of the few written for the many. It cannot even be the pulling together of individual ideas into consensus. Instead, shared leadership emerges from a focused set of goals and a common commitment. People are committed to one another and to seeing the work completed. We are bound together to the realization of the vision.

Building shared leadership begins with our profound dreams and deepest individual hopes. It also begins as we confess to one another our own lack of vision, wavering commitment, dim hopes, and lost dreams. Shared leadership begins with taking the logs out of our own eyes before we venture forth to look for the specks in our sisters' or brothers' eyes. As we proceed, we will transcend our limitations to find a wholeness and a connection, a shared expression of life experience we might have missed in going it alone.

Getting (and Keeping) the Big Picture

Affirmation: I not only survive but also thrive with the vision of wholeness before me.

"From the day I entered the door of my new job, I could sense it. I was suspect. The unwritten code was: 'Don't trust. We do not trust you. Prove yourself worthy of our trust. Show us why we should have confidence in you and then—maybe—we'll consider.'" Dale confided after two months on the job.

Many of us have experienced organizations that operate from the defensive posture of distrust. We feel their judgment breathing down our necks. The attitude hangs like smog. Newcomers are seen as enemies to be distrusted until we traverse some mysterious maze that supposedly leads to trust.

Their mazes go nowhere. There is no trust. Places of employment that harbor this attitude are hard, if not impossible, for the spiritual person to work in. Everyday trials inflict constant spiritual wounds. Betrayal is particularly awful, because it shakes our confidence in our own judgment. People ask, "How could I have been so blind? How could I have been such a fool?" We become frustrated at the barriers that keep us from functioning as the leaders we know we are.

Trust or Distrust, That Is the Question

This is not to say that all people should be equally trusted. There are some things I would not tell Stephen, my seven year old, and trust him to keep silent about. Allowing for his maturity level, I share with him certain levels of information. I might tell him about a present I bought for his dad's birthday. In this case, a slip of the tongue in his excitement would not be the end of the world. But I would not tell him confidential information about my life. This is not to place judgment upon him, but only to recognize and accept who he is and what information he is capable of keeping in confidence. To give him highly confidential information that he does not have the maturity to handle would be unloving. It would be unfair to him and a betrayal of myself.

In other relationships, as with my child, I begin at the point of trust. I work with and relate to persons in trust until they show me that they are not yet ready to be trusted. I once told a confidence to a good friend. She in turn shared it with another one of my friends, judging that this would be all right. She did not understand that I had given her a trusted gift. I trusted her not to share it with another person. I felt betrayed and asked her about it. She apologized, and I forgave her. My forgiveness was genuine. The friend who revealed my secret to a third party may not have been gossiping, but she surely had betrayed my trust. I realize that I cannot continue to trust her with the same confidences after she has demonstrated her incapability to hold that trust. To do so would be the equivalent of shooting myself in the foot. It would be self-sabotage.

When forty-year-old Nina's sister was dying of AIDS last year, Nina took on the responsibility for her care. She was determined to fulfill her sister's wish to die at home while continuing to work in her high-pressure sales job with a major Chicago firm. "I kept up with my work load through it all," she said, "and it was my job that kept me sane." Toward the end, Nina asked her boss for extra help with some of her accounts. "I needed more flexibility in my working hours, and she was understanding. At first she wanted to give me time off. I explained to her that I needed to keep working for my own mental well-being. My boss respected my privacy and kept the information to herself, sharing it with colleagues only as needed for office management. I came to a point when I had to trust that she would use discretion. I was not disappointed.

It is freeing to realize that some people are capable and others simply are incapable of returning the trust we offer. Their abilities or inabilities have nothing to do with us. We can, with gratitude, thank the former for being the trusting persons that they are. We can let go of the resentment and anger we've felt toward the latter and accept them for who they are. We do not expect them to offer a trust that is beyond their capabilities and do not place that burden upon them.

Why should we trust in our relationships, especially in the places where we work? If you share your life with others, there is one thing you can count on: You will be let down. Yes, sometimes there are painful consequences as we share our lives and risk any level of intimacy. But giving up on relationships is not the answer. If love and trust rule our relationships, we make certain decisions about our relationships in order to remain in them. The fundamental question is not whether we *trust* each other, but whether we *love* each other. To love *and* to trust is the only choice if we are to be in co-creation with each other. This is what God intends. It is as we live in trust that we can live in mutuality with others. As we are empowered to work together, instead of going it alone, we are freed to do only what God has called us to do within God's time and will for our life.

Giving Up Illusions of Control

Walking in faith is hard, but it is the only way we can truly live. It takes a lot of faith to live one day at a time. Living faithfully, fully in faith each day may be difficult, but it is the only way to be truly alive. The alternative, building a wall around our hearts to keep from being hurt or thinking we can control everything that happens, or that we can be God, is arrogant!

When we anticipate God's Spirit working in our lives like yeast mixed in flour, we discover new qualities for leadership rising within ourselves. We uncover powers and ideas that unleash our imaginations in new ways. We find many resources on which to draw and begin to trust our abilities as we move into new arenas. We are transformed and led to new heights of freedom when we use our best abilities in all we undertake. Like poet Emily Dickinson, we "dwell in possibility."

Chaos: Precondition for New Life

Effective leaders are willing to function in the midst of creative chaos. They learn how to feel at home with life's natural chaos. Not only our jobs, but also our marriages, friendships, parenting, and all relationships are given over to chaos from time to time. Only in this way can they be renewed and created again.

Did you know that some leaders feel it is their God-given duty to do away with all chaos? In fact, they feel called to eliminate anything that is not "in order" as they understand it. For them, disorder must be erased. They define disorder as innovation, dissension, creativity, change, or challenge. You see it manifested in the leader's life by the memos, multiplication of paper, personnel manuals, by-laws and rigidity of rules. Some clergy take to a new plane their vows of "word, sacrament and order," heavy on the order! Oh, and in some arenas, leaders enthusiastically quote the governing manual, page and paragraph. Well-intentioned leaders become imprisoning rather than empowering.

I often remind myself that chaos is a precondition for new life. God created life out of death—a new order. In Genesis, the beginning, creation comes out of chaos. Any institution or organization that doesn't have a measure of chaos is half dead. If your business, institution, or congregation doesn't have some chaos, then there's nothing happening. Many leaders I've spoken to laughingly assure me that there is a lot happening!

Let's face it. It is difficult to move forward in the midst of chaos. It is frustrating when we feel helpless to effect the final outcome. It is like slogging through deep mud to move from action to waiting. Instead of facing our inability to control, we deny it. We think we can overcome feelings of helplessness if we try harder, manipulate more skillfully, and scheme more cleverly. We force love with all our might, but it's not enough. We do all we can to change the circumstances, and nothing works. Some of us have had dreams all our lives, and now we realize that they will never become reality. Others of us come to a pivotal opportunity in our lives, but because of circumstances and responsibilities have to let the opportunity go by. One day all our struggling and striving fail as we come face to face with our powerlessness. All the manuals on leadership tell us how to take control. But none prepare us to be leaders who can live with powerlessness.

The Root of Our Drive Is Fear

What lies below the stem of our drive for order? It is the same root of our destructive life journey. The root is our fear and denial of death. Death is seen as the ultimate chaos, the ultimate enemy. Comedian Woody Allen says it so aptly for us: "I'm not afraid of dying, I just don't want to be there when it happens!"

We are all going to die. When we acknowledge this reality, we can face the fact that "since I am going to die, since I don't have forever, in fact I only have today, I might as well live it to its fullest!" From that point on, death has no power over us. The gates of hell cannot prevail against us. I vividly recall the moment in my own life when I realized that there was nothing "they" could give me or take away from me. In that moment, I was freed to be who I am. I no longer had to please or check each of my decisions and actions against the backdrop of the grand prize "they" could grant me. I had to work through the seduction of thinking that the system could ultimately make me or break me. The system does not have that power. A passage from Scripture holds this reality to the light: "I am convinced that neither death, nor life, nor angels, nor rulers, nor things present, nor things to come, nor powers, nor height, nor depth, nor anything else in all creation, will be able to separate us from the love of God . . . No, in all these things we are more than conquerors through [God] who loved us!"

No wonder our bosses are so frightened of us when we live in this reality. We begin to live in joy, letting go of our embeddedness, preconceived notions, drivenness, and in-culturations. Our new selves are ready for grand adventure. We are ready, as someone expressed it, to find our bliss and follow it. Power-keepers would prefer that we stay in line, held in bondage, keeping our eyes on the prize.

Death Is Not the Enemy

For believers, death has no unbreakable hold on us. I believe that when we die we are propelled into a life of infinite beauty, greater possibilities, and extended horizons. We will dance into an indescribably wonderful destiny. Thank goodness the psalmist does not minimize death when he writes: "Yea, though I walk through the valley of the shadow of death, I will fear no evil." This psalm does not ask us to pretend that death and evil do not exist. It simply states that fear is not a part of the picture. It does not have the power to make us afraid to live. Death is a natural cycle of life and not the enemy. As we become leaders who encompass life and accept death, we will discover that mystery in our depths frees us to live fully today.

In our businesses, institutions, and organizations we fear the chaos of death. We keep alive projects, committees, and systems that have been in a coma and on life-support systems for years. The need to learn how to die is a central message in the spiritual journey. No, not in the literal physical sense, but in the spiritual part of ourselves. Scripture tells us that those who try to make their life secure will lose it, but those who lose their life will keep it, for to live is Christ (that vision of wholeness), and to die is gain!

If you want to free people to take action, then you need to communicate that you know many new endeavors will not succeed, and that's okay. One of the biggest obstacles in our lives is fear of failure. We are not to be perfect. Because something is unsuccessful does not mean that we, the initiators, are failures. We see change and disequilibrium as a friend rather than as a foe. Disorder and instability are necessary for new life to emerge in institutions and even in our personal lives. Encourage those you lead to entertain new thoughts and ideas. Suggest that they invite their new ideas in for a cup of coffee. They don't have to marry every one of them! When we are willing to risk, to set aside our fear and do the best we can, the barriers will dissolve and constrictions will disappear. When we trust, the future will be filled with wondrous expressions and tremendous experiences. It may surprise us, but we really can survive and even thrive with chaos around us. How many of us are willing to swing from rope to rope into what appears to be chaos, trusting that the next rope will appear when it is time?

Touch the Future in Faith

It takes faith to live one day at a time, trusting that God's Spirit will continue with us no matter what. Many of us quell the Spirit's urgings because we fear anything new or different. We fear what makes us feel vulnerable. It is arrogant to think that we can control everything that happens. We have illusions that we can control situations, other persons' lives, or the future. We can't. We do our homework, make the best decisions we can, then trust and live in the uncertainty of life. We become fully alive as we learn to live in trust.

Our inner spirit urges us to touch the future in trust. When we take time to listen to another person or teach someone a new concept, we do much more than transfer information; we share our trust in tomorrow. When we pray in the midst of chaos and the storms of life, we open ourselves to new possibilities. When we awaken our senses to new understandings, study a new concept, or meet new friends and associates, we grow and are beckoned toward new horizons. Our fears still come and go, but we are able to move through them as we trust the Spirit. We grow as we listen to our inner guide. Fearlessly, without anxiety or ambition, we thrive as we trust the inner journey and move into that vision of wholeness. To survive means to merely live or exist. Spirit-filled leaders thrive!

Take a time of quiet, more than just a moment, and read this affirmation slowly several times until it becomes your own.

Today I give up my illusions of control. I hand over my drivenness that leads to functional atheism. I cannot control situations, others' lives, or the future. In the past I tried to control situations until I managed to force the outcome I desired. Later I realized that this outcome failed to offer the happiness I'd hoped for. I wish now that I had heeded the clues, recognizing that what I sought was not the Spirit's leading after all. I now know that when I force into manifestation what I want, ignoring what God wants, I usually end up with something other than what I'd truly longed for. Today I take a leap of faith and embrace the uncertainty of life, knowing that I walk in certainty in the Spirit's presence.

Doing Spiritwork

Affirmation: I can learn to lead from a new
spiritual center.

To lead, first you need to know how to live from a
new spiritual center. To walk in the rapture of being
fully alive is to be completely awake, with eyes wide
open and senses alert to the possibilities of each
day. The Spirit-centered leader strives to be totally conscious and, as much as possible, self-aware in each waking
moment. This fully conscious state of being comes as we
experience a power that is greater than ourselves. Acknowledgment of the transcendent is central to becoming an
effective leader. This transcendent power of life moves us
beyond our fears to a greater freedom. It allows us to
exceed our own human limitations.

When I speak of a new spiritual center, I am not simply
talking about people who are psychologically well adjusted.
A centeredness of the human spirit is much more than
mental stability. Leaders who are spiritually centered have
an overarching vision of life greater than any problem they
might encounter. This vantage point frees them from the
need to force the agenda. The natural processes of life and
human interactions are allowed to take their course. This

encounter with the very being of God enables leaders to live in holy, respectful ways. They see the divine presence in each person they meet. Their reality is that God is alive within themselves and others.

Effective leaders recognize that management by objective and manipulated organizational structures has not gotten them where they've wanted to go. They have moved outside mental fences and lifestyle traps even as they continue to work within their systems. Goals and objectives are not the measure of their success.

This experience of God within is not something you can make happen. But you can prepare yourself to receive the gift when it is given. The best things cannot be told in words; they can only be lived. As they are experienced, we can then know them and name them. And even that naming is a feeble attempt to clothe the transcendent in language, which is never adequate. It is that vast ground of mystery that we all share. It is the knowledge of a greater truth.

Encountering the Transcendent

When I speak of the transcendent, I am talking about a journey, not into the intellect and the mind, but into an understanding that is beyond what we presently know and comprehend. I am not talking about how we spend our days or the external value we place on tasks and duties. Instead, I am talking about who we will be as we go about our daily life.

There are two ways people encounter the transcendent. The first way is through a lifelong process. Persons intentionally place themselves in circumstances that encourage growth and exploration. They take the necessary time to cultivate the spirit within their own lives. Their stories demonstrate time spent in the school of hard knocks. They venture over the abyss and emerge solid within themselves. Standing firm, they keep their center when everything else around them is shaking. Persons easily identified who have chosen this journey include Mahatma Gandhi, Mother Teresa, and Martin Luther King, Jr.

Choosing the higher road paid off for thirty-year-old Adair when she was fired from her job as assistant vice president of a medical supply company. Adair knew when she moved into the management position that there was a possibility that her position would be in jeopardy, but she weighed her need for a new challenge and decided to take the risk. After a take over, Adair's new boss brought in his own management team. Adair was devastated because she had worked so hard, and she was disappointed, because she was leaving unfinished projects to which she had personally given a great deal of vision and energy. Still, she made every effort to give her replacement the benefit of her experience during the three-week transition period.

"My first impulse was to leave right away," she recalls, "maybe take my computer records. But I took time out to think about what that would accomplish—other than creating enemies. The strength to do what was right came from knowing that in the grand scheme of things it is better to take the high road. I may not have to work with these people in the future, but I would have to live with myself. Because I was spiritually centered when the tough times came, I was able to leave the company with a strong sense of well-being. My replacement turned out to be a very decent woman, and she made a point of telling her boss how helpful I'd been to her.

The boss wrote a glowing recommendation and networked me with some other contacts in his company. As a result, I found a new position in less than two weeks. Later in the year, my successor invited me to lunch and told me she had never seen anyone behave with such class as I did during the transition. I had never thought of my actions as being classy—I thought it was in my best interest. It gave me a sense

*of esteem to behave well when I had been treated
shabbily. Now I'm a stronger person, ready to take
the next risk, knowing I have the spiritual resources
I'll need for future opportunities.*

Class. Dignity. Grace under fire. Whatever you call it,
Adair is an example of what it means to struggle through
hardships and stand strong. When times are tough, the
people who come through best are those who manage to
see themselves as more than the sum of their troubles.
Even in the worst of circumstances, they don't define or
present themselves as victims.

Adair would not compare herself to Gandhi, Mother
Teresa, or Martin Luther King, Jr. But perhaps she, like
them, not only survived but also thrived because she found
a hope that reached higher than her own limited mental,
psychological, and physical resources allowed. Each of
them met the transcendent power face to face. They had
an encounter with the Divine Spirit.

The second way people encounter the transcendent is
not a chosen way. Instead, it is placed upon them in a
traumatic, life-changing event that altered the very fabric
of who they are. Their deepest fears have been realized.
They thought they would die, physically and spiritually,
but they are still alive. It takes time to heal the deep
wounds, but in the end they survive and thrive. Like small
children who timidly cross the street for the first time to
discover a whole new city block, they discover new worlds
they never knew existed. These encounters with the abyss
may include the death of a loved one; betrayal by a friend;
a traumatic, life-changing experience such as an accident
or physical disability; a serious illness; or a near-death
experience. For some people, the loss of vocation is that
life-altering encounter. Here we speak not of changing jobs
or moving to a new location but of the inability of a person
to continue in any manner with the work he or she loves
and has given his or her life to.

This was the third birthday I had spent without Sherry and my son. I knew from past experience that it would be a tearful day for me, just as holidays and their birthdays were always mixed with sadness, hard for me to bear without them.

And yet, despite my loneliness and pain, I have managed to go on with my life. One day, I finally realized that as helpful as friends and family had been, I was the one who would have to "do it" for me. I had to find faith and courage within myself. Reaching deep inside myself, and with the help of God, I found the strength—a strength I never knew existed. It was this determination to begin again and build some sort of life for myself that has brought me to where I stand today.

Perhaps it could be better, but given what life has dealt me, it's been a good place to be. I've had my health, physically and mentally, and I've managed to open a business, become self-supporting, and keep my home.

Tim's life took a different course when his wife and son were killed in a head-on collision. Once the barrier had been crossed, reality was changed forever. Going back to his previously manageable world was not an option. Tim found the strength of the Spirit within in order to go on.

Through intentional seeking on the person's part or through life-altering events—either way, transcendence is encountered, and life's perspective is forever changed. Life will never again be the same. Transcending the difficulties of life, the effective leader calls upon the Spirit's strength within to move forward into the future with a new clearness of vision.

Distinguishing Marks of the Effective Transcendent Leader

Effective, Spirit-filled leaders who have experienced the transcendent God possess distinguishing traits. Consider nine listed here.

1. Connecting with the mystery of life, they know it is manifested in all things. Their vision is one that encompasses a unity with all of creation.
2. They have come face to face with the transcendent in their own lives. They acknowledge a power and rule beyond themselves that supersedes their own small world. Holding a sense of the "otherness" of the universe, they experience, this "other" within themselves and within the people with whom they work.
3. They understand time in the linear sense differently because they have experienced their own mortality. They see their life in the grander scheme of creation and all human time.
4. Living within their own power through the Divine Spirit, they move beyond living life in ordinary ways. For leaders to be truly effective means for them to move from their own opinions and intellect to the mystery of what it means to be fully alive.
5. Spiritually centered, they do not say no to the parts of life they find uncomfortable. Instead, they embrace the entirety of life with all its joy and pain.
6. Because their identity does not depend on a temporary role, they do not allow the possibility of losing their position or job to make them fearful.
7. They do not work through a transference of neediness or a drivenness for power for its own sake. Power is sought only as it can empower and give aid to others.
8. They know how to live and have no need to control or manipulate other people or circumstances. This allows them to accept colleagues, family, and friends as they are, not expecting them to be people they cannot be.
9. Spirit-filled leaders discover the presence of the holy within themselves and the people in their business, company, or institution. They lead people out of captivity to a "new home."

The Heart and Soul of Leadership

Scores of leadership theories flood the market. I reviewed many of them as I was preparing to speak to a convention of leaders. Some are straightforward business formulas. Others are the "flavors of the month," the same information marketed in a new package. Still more show gimmicky follow-my-formula-for-success models. We may wish we could ignore some of their theories and influence on leaders in our workplaces, but we cannot. These models for leadership, some based on faulty assumptions, have a bearing on our lives. They also contain useful teachings that help us sharpen our own leadership styles. Certainly many espouse values and moral systems that are good when lived out.

Yet, I've often found that an ingredient is missing from these leadership books. These authors fail to address what lies within and beyond the techniques. They do not speak to what makes leaders more than technicians able to manage. They fail to speak to us as people who have hearts and souls. They ignore the spiritual dimension, which nurtures all aspects of life. Leaders need the missing ingredient when faced with overwhelming tasks and responsibilities.

William's boss is a good example of a leader who cares for the spiritual needs of her employees.

When forty-seven-year-old William discovered he had cancer and was to undergo treatment, he was determined to continue handling a high-pressure position as a graphic artist with an advertising firm. "I didn't miss a deadline during those weeks," he says, "and I think the work helped me take the needed breaks from my own troubles.

"I did go to my boss to ask if colleagues could sit in on some of my meetings. She gave me more flexibility in my work hours and relieved me of some of my workload. She couldn't have been more sympathetic. I told her I needed to keep working, that it

wouldn't help either me or my family if I didn't. She really touched me once when she said she would be sure to lift up my name in prayer at the Sunday worship service of her congregation. Do you know that when people see you doing your best, they come through for you in the most amazing ways?"

If we are leaders who lead by the Spirit, who have the gift of hope and clear vision, then how do we get sidetracked? Why can't we stay focused? Is it because we are asked to do so many other things that seem needed and important? Do we slip into routines, seduced into continuing the same bureaucracy as those who preceded us? It is tempting to simply "please the customer," selling our management wares in tidy packages for quick consumption. Instead, leaders are asked to live in chaos—in the places where sickness finds healing, the cursed find blessing, and darkness meets light. This healing-blessing-light happens under the surface, behind the scenes. If we get all caught up in minding the business, who will be the leader?

The souls of leaders hunger and thirst. We sense an inner emptiness, a void, a chasm within ourselves that forever calls out in starvation. This inner ache reminds us that we possess a spirit. Most of the time we neglect this place that lives within us. We try to fill the hunger with running meetings, writing memos, and returning calls. But every so often the emptiness grabs our attention and tells us it will not be so easily ignored.

The failure of leaders to deal with their own inner lives is deeply troubling, not only for themselves, but also for others in the misery they create. We cannot continue in this way. We who wish to lead from a new spiritual center cannot allow the business managers of the world to set our agenda for leadership. As people longing to uncover the inner journey, we seek guideposts to cultivate the sacredness and depth of everyday life. How? Through Spiritwork.

Spiritwork as Spiritual Formation

On the main street in the small town of Lemoyne, Pennsylvania, you can visit Body Work. There you can make an appointment to have body work done on yourself. You can get yourself realigned, have your spine adjusted, get your system cleansed, and your feet reflexed. Your body, these gurus tout, will be "centered." We who lead from the Spirit need to adopt and respect getting our priorities realigned, our attitude adjusted, our souls restored, and our vision expanded. We need Spiritwork.

Spiritwork is different from body work in that it is not something you can pay to have done to you. Spiritwork is opening oneself to God's work within. When we open ourselves we are formed by the Spirit and conformed to the image of divine love. This is known as "spiritual formation." There is a strong power at work in us today. Its presence empowers us to do far more with our lives than we ever dreamed possible. We don't have to work through our own intellect or ability to draw love from some external source. We set aside our notions of God as some old man with a long white beard out there someplace in the sky. Why waste energy on a pie-in-the-sky theology? Constant love is readily available to us here and now. As we tap into this flow of power, we have energy to lead those we are called to serve.

A word of warning: Take care not to change Spiritwork into another form of "self-improvement." The problem with self-improvement articles and books is that they imply there is something terribly wrong with us. They dwell on our warts instead of our beauty marks. There is a difference between self-improvement and the unfolding of the Spirit. Self-improvement can easily be measured by prescribed outcomes and goals. It asks for perfection. Spiritwork is revealed when the Spirit is at work within and you become more open to what life has to offer. It invites you to become more fully the person you are growing to be. The work of the Spirit does not call for perfection, but for a journey. You live life with a freshness and a vitality not experienced before.

Deep spiritual work happens only with time set aside for that purpose. Spiritual work is as important as any task or project. This work of the *in* and *down* is as crucial as any outer work we do. Today we slow down and do not feel guilty about "wasting time." Spiritwork cannot be ventured into at a brisk pace. The Spirit travels at an unhurried tempo. Therefore, to build a Spirit-centered life you will need to move with patience and remain loyal to the searching and probing. This thoughtful pace is not understood in our workaday world of "I want it yesterday." Indeed, we take care lest we make the mistake of approaching Spiritwork in a way that does not have spiritual light.

The Fruits of Leadership

The holy Scriptures hold a beautiful description of how we will know when we are living and leading in the Spirit. There are clear evidences that we can sense for ourselves. It reads, "The fruit of the Spirit is love, joy, peace, patience, kindness, generosity, faithfulness, gentleness and self-control. . . . If we live by the Spirit, let us also be guided by the Spirit." I invite you to put these "fruits" into your leadership.

• **Love** is expressed as I take the time to laugh and share a moment of humor with a colleague.

• **Joy** comes when I know that I am loved and, in return, I am loving.

• **Peace** is mine when I live each day, one day at a time.

• **Patience** is within me when I wait in hope and expectation, knowing all will be well.

• **Kindness** is present as I give the benefit of the doubt to another person.

• **Generosity** is known when I give my time to help a co-worker.

• **Faithfulness** is lived as I continue to struggle for consensus and understanding.

75

• **Gentleness** is a keystone in my life when I take the effort to walk in another's shoes.
• **Self-control** is displayed when I make decisions that are helpful to my life and to my community.

Those of us who are guided by the Spirit will lead by the Spirit! These Spiritwork guides come only in glimpses. For a little while, the scales fall from our eyes. We actually see the holiness and beauty and mystery of the world and the people around us. Then, from deep down restoration comes; our inner emptiness is filled. We can't make it happen. We can't make it last. It comes upon us as a glimpse, a whisper, and we grab the rope.

Community Is Central

Spiritwork is a deeply personal matter, but not always a private matter. In fact, community is central in our swing up and out. The swing into the unknown can be so precarious and frightening that we need the company of others who have traveled the path before us. While we teeter on the edge of the tower, staring at the abyss, we bond with one another in Spiritwork.

I'm grateful for all the people who have guided me and shared in my times of searching and pain. Through these interactions, I have found healing—physically, emotionally, and spiritually. With such companions, we share our ongoing stories—the struggles and the victories. Community support teaches us to use our love and enthusiasm to become more caring and compassionate.

When Richard, my first husband, died at the age of twenty-nine, I was only twenty-five. I was fearful of letting anyone else come too close. Pastoring a congregation at the time, I wanted to prove I was a strong spiritual leader. I was unable to allow others to lead me through this dark valley. I often found myself comforting other people. Somewhere deep inside, I stuffed my own sadness and weariness. Over seven years I had built a tough shell in order to care for a sick husband. Watching at his bedside for six weeks as he slipped away left me numb. I could not face the reality of his death. Throughout the days after his burial, I lived in the terror of the sobs that began in the empty part of my stomach, worked their way up into my throat, and lodged there. I was suffocating. There were days when I thought I'd go crazy, nights when I knew that I had. I could not share my pain, because I feared it would overwhelm me. Other people would see my grief and think me faithless. Lord forbid! They would know I was human!

Now I look back and rejoice over the wonderful people who were there even when I didn't know I needed them. This was particularly true in my times of utter darkness. They helped me out of darkness into light. Today, they remain my partners, soulmates, colleagues, and best friends. They continue to bring a rich supply of blessings and a wealth of inspiration for me to be the best I can be. I gratefully acknowledge these friends, realizing that my life would not be as whole without their presence. They are supportive, but not invasive. They walk with me on the edge of the abyss, neither rescuing me nor filling the air with platitudes or advice.

Think about your own spiritual community. Who has been a healer for you? For whom are you a healer? These special friends are important not only in our personal lives but also in our professional lives. It is difficult to lead in healthy ways if we are not, ourselves, healthy persons.

A Call for Responsibility, Accountability, and Discipline

Leaders ask one another: "Does my behavior reflect my beliefs?" "Am I living the values I profess?" We help one another search for solutions. Through others, we subject our assumptions to reality checks on our journey to integrity. When we love and support one another, we actively call for responsibility, accountability, and discipline.

This community of friends accompanies us in ways that respect us and help us to step to the edge and stretch our spiritual nerve in faith while we reach for the next rope.

We need community for the journey of Spiritwork. It is too great a distance to swing out alone.

Five Basic Works of the Spirit

There are five works of the Spirit that have been helpful to me as I've learned how to bend toward the mystery, to lead by the inward and downward journey, to fill my soul. I have named them (1) integrating ourselves, (2) reaching intimacy, (3) connecting body and spirit, (4) seeking soulful souls, and (5) naming reality. The remaining chapters will address these five Spiritworks in detail.

Holy Space

First, however, is the need to create holy space to make way for the Spirit to work. Aaron's case offers a good example of this principle.

Aaron felt stressed, sensing that people thought him incompetent. He wondered if his integrity was in question. When the concern was raised by his superior, his anxiety was compounded. Aaron received a memo from his boss with wording that was fuzzy and indirect. The memo said one thing, but he sensed there was an underlying connotation. Aaron knew there was an edge of truth to the charge, or at least enough to cause him to doubt himself. No one's motives are ever completely pure, and all workers experience days when they aren't quite on top. Aaron was no exception.

Aaron's panic button was pushed. His stomach twisted into knots, making him physically ill. In his anxiety, he would spring to action, doing damage control, playing the "fix-it" person in the situation. He would write the perfect memo to counter the perceived attack. He would run around covering whatever he thought would correct the situation.

Now Aaron takes a different course. When he feels

overwhelmed, he closes his door, backs off from his rigorous daily schedule, and slows down. He distances himself from the situation, thus lowering his anxiety. This helps to bring the problem into a manageable perspective. He uses a break or lunch time to walk away from the building. Other times he goes into the bathroom and simply closes the door.

What can you do in a similar situation? Measure whether the situation requires immediate action or response. Most situations don't. Take the time, days if possible, to calm down and put the situation in perspective. Is this something that really warrants a crisis mentality? Or are you some dysfunctional person's running target? Gather all the information and advice you can. Sleep on your decision. In the evening after a difficult day, allow yourself time to loaf, to notice your surroundings and to speak with God. Center this restful time on health and healing. Taking time to relax, meditate, and pray is vital to your spiritual well-being. Trust yourself to listen. Allow the Spirit to work in and through you.

When you are in tune with the Spirit's work, your inner voice is calm. You can more quickly set aside the feelings of panic and settle back into your sense of confidence and peace. You open yourself to grow in strength and love. You are able to care for yourself and lead in gentle ways, directing caring actions instead of reactionary negative actions toward others.

In these moments of quiet, we do not worry when our mind wanders or about the quality of the prayer. We simply pray, reflect, and meditate and know that our time is well spent. Times of prayer and reflection help us to perform our leadership role more competently, lovingly, honestly, and confidently. Prayer is truly a gift, for it helps us to sort out life's complications and strengthens our connections to God and to other people.

Spiritwork keeps us from panic. We do not let the uncertainty of tomorrow overshadow today. Neither do we let the promises of tomorrow cause us to forget the possibilities of today. We live in the present moment. We slow down, look around, and observe what we are doing and why we are doing it. Guided by wisdom, we live today to its fullest and take tomorrow in stride.

When thought patterns grow cluttered and our sense of purpose becomes fuzzy and unclear, it is time to pause and determine why. It is important to step back from the problems of our work and look at them from a reflective perspective. I have three questions that I use to judge the importance of any event or seeming crisis. They have a way of putting things in perspective.

1. Is anyone dying? (With my history, that is a valid question.)
2. Will this be important five years from now?
3. Who else will be affected by this?

For a better vantage point, you need to make an appointment to sit in silence and listen carefully. Finding a quiet space and time to reflect on and refocus is important. You need to create "holy space" for times of reflection—space where you step back from the busyness and clamor to hear what God has to say. Spreading out your cluttered agenda in front of you, allow God to sort it out and find clearer answers than you could find on your own.

Prayerfulness or Prayerlessness?

Prayer time is essential, as necessary as eating and sleeping—important enough to write the appointment on your calendar and keep it. This is not wasting time. Production may not be immediately visible to your board of directors, supervisor or boss, but it is there. Your colleagues, associates, and co-workers will thank you.

When we fail to take this time, the results can be literally numbing. We make ourselves stop feeling so that we can make it through the day. We move through days on automatic pilot. Without prayer, our journey becomes a struggle. We grow discontent. We don't want to be the walking dead!

But when we seek solitude and answer the cry of our spirits, we find needed nourishment. We create an inner environment in which meditative, reflective prayerfulness can breathe. We take time to experience all of our emotions, thoughts, and deepest longings. "The glory of God is the human being fully alive," the great saint Ireneas wrote. Prayer is time spent being present with and conscious of our Creator. We find strength to live, not dazed and half asleep, but fully awake. We discover our strength within and emerge back into the world, responding fully to the rich possibilities for service and leadership that life offers.

The decision is between a life of prayerfulness and an existence of prayerlessness. Living a life of prayer and reflection means that we:

• experience the divine energy of the Spirit's vitality and flourish as leaders;
• make room for God's greater will to act in and through us;
• face our inner self, no longer afraid of being alone;
• learn to live the mystery of God and let go of our own obsessive control;
• know who we are as persons of worth and holiness;
• envision what it means to live mutually, connected and in community;
• work to disarm our functional atheism and drivenness to lead in freeing, empowering ways;
• claim our own power as we co-create with others;
• take down dividing walls and learn to trust again;
• keep the vision up front and know that we will survive, even when all seems chaotic.

Pause as you have time in your reading and reflect. I invite you to take the time you need in meditation and prayerfulness to wrestle with three questions:

Am I ready to swing out over the abyss, trusting the voice?

Can I make the journey down and in?

81

Learning to Lead from Your Spiritual Center

Am I ready to meet the terror that lies inside so that I can be the kind of leader needed by God today?

Pause, reflect, and be in the presence of the holy with the following prayer:

Lover God, you have called me to lead in this time and place. I want to be ready. Help me to be what you intend me to be and to do what you want me to do. I know that the cost is high, especially against the backdrop of what is happening in many organizations. Who wants to journey down and into the depths? But there is no other choice if I am to be the loving, co-creating leader you call me to be.

I pray that this is not just another reading for entertainment, but that you can break through and in and down; that I would find your Spirit once again. Part of me is ready; another part of me wants to escape. Please break through that I might open myself to Spiritwork, swing free from the madding crowd and over the abyss to lead your people home. Amen.

Getting Through the Tough Times

Spiritwork: Integrating ourselves

Ted tries to be a reasonable person. Each day he awakens, knowing that certain things are expected of him. The cats, kids, and turtles need to be fed. His boss expects him to show up at work. He has responsibilities to meet and duties to perform. Ted believes he is a rational, reasonable person who functions from a certain set of values and knowledge of how the world functions and his place in its workings. Right? Now he's not so sure—at least not about the rational, reasonable part.

There are days when he rebels. The kids eat peanut butter and jelly; the pets fast for a day; and he calls in sick. Being a single parent is no treat. There has to be more to life than this! He simply can't face another day of work. So he calls a halt. He quits! Well, not really. He reminds himself that he can't afford to quit. That would mean a terrible financial burden he is not ready to assume. It would mean the necessity of letting go of financial goals. To quit means to jeopardize his house, the kids' tuition, his pension, and the children's new school clothes. Besides, his work itself—if you can side-step all the office shenanigans—is important to him. On better days, he enjoys what he does. He knows he can't quit. So he gets his body out of bed and drags himself to work.

Sticking Through the Hard Times

My work is important to me. It is also enjoyable. The one thing I've learned, working in a factory assembly line or getting stuck on an island in a typhoon during a business trip, is how to make work a fun adventure. When past jobs became mere labor, a career move or only a moneymaking proposition, it was either time to move on or to face burn out. Even in my present vocation, I'm hard pressed to call it labor. I love the things I do—teaching, speaking, mentoring, and planning. I don't even mind a bit of administration. It's a delight to see the pile of papers recede from my desk as letters are answered, questionnaires are returned, and bills are paid. I'm amazed, and often reminded by the finance office, that I have a pay check to pick up. "You mean they pay me for this, too?"

The reason why I stick with a job through the tough times is because of the joy of the vocation itself and finding my place in the larger scheme of life. If I allowed my work to be dictated entirely by money, advancement in the hierarchy, hunger for fame, or the need to please others, I would be fooling myself. I know, from experience, that there is a time when it doesn't matter what I'm paid, what impressive title I can print on business cards, or what prizes are dangled in front of me. When the time comes that the joy is gone, so am I.

I'm not talking about bailing out when I disagree with the boss, have differences of opinions with co-workers, or receive assignments that are not my choice. All jobs have their daily grind and impossible people. I stick with my job through the hard times because I sense that I am where I am supposed to be. I have a deep commitment to God's work in my life and hold that perspective, knowing that the trials of today prepare me for the challenges of tomorrow. I see my work as part of a grander scheme for the universe.

In order to stick it out through the hard times, there are four things you need to grasp:

1. Be alert to the line between a commitment to healthy Spirit-centered leadership and an attachment to unhealthy, ego-enhancing projects.

2. Create space where you and others can discover and experience God's fulfillment. This releases you from all the "oughts" and "shoulds" laid on you, encumbering your journey.

3. Follow your heart's desire. If you can't find a way to work in an enjoyable fashion, do yourself and everyone else a favor and don't do it! When you attend to what your heart tells you, you draw closest to what God intends. When the Spirit guides your use of time and energy, you experience a refreshing spontaneity and commitment.

4. Have compassion for others. Carry light to dark places, give a lift to burdens, bring water in a desert, share touch with the hurting spirit, and accord concern and constant care over the long haul.

Compartmentalization Versus Wholeness

"Experts" tell us not to bring our work problems home. We're to "leave it at the office." But that is easier said than done. In fact, we can't. If the high stress levels in our colleagues are any indication, they too are unable to turn off some mysterious switch and walk away. It is perhaps a myth that we can divide ourselves into compartments, saying, "This is the person I am at work, and this other person is who I am at home." Trying to put your working life into one compartment and your private life into another does not work. Don't get me wrong. There are times when a healthy dose of "It is the weekend, and it will be here when I get back" is needed. Like dishes left in the sink, the work will still be there when you return. We all need vacations and some three-day weekends.

People who divide themselves scare me. If they can cut a part of themselves off at will, then what else are they capable of? Wouldn't we rather have a leader who is the same person at work that she or he is at home? This person is not divided, but a whole person. We need leaders who are thoroughly integrated, and we need to be leaders who are integrated.

The Case of Eli

Eli's wife shared this comment: "Eli used to be fun loving at home. He was a warm and open man. Known for his generosity, he was responsive to my emotional needs. He was gentle and compassionate with the kids. I say was, because lately he seems distant from both the kids and me. In fact, he's never home. Eli says that it is just as easy to stay at the office and work late as it is to drag files home. He sees his family on weekends and then only if he's not on the road. The kids are almost grown and gone. I just don't know what happened to the Eli I once knew. Where did he go?"

As a young CEO, Eli was known for his collegiality, support, and friendliness. He was a warm person, open to new ideas and other people's leadership. As the years passed, so did Eli's openness. Somewhere along the way he cut himself off. Now he sticks to the regulations in the personnel and policy manuals, ruling by the letter of the law. When situations or people seem to get out of his control, he creates new policies with the use of rubber-stamp committees and memos. Once in a while, his workers sense him trying to communicate. These efforts always prove to be false starts, and the wall goes up once again.

In the beginning, Eli unconsciously lived by two separate sets of guidelines. He was able to "go with the flow" of family life, to give and take as needed. Fun loving and affectionate, he played the role of the "Leave It to Beaver" father. At the office he became another person. He took on the role of business executive extraordinaire. Trying to display an openness, instead he was rigid, sticking to the rules, no matter what the cost. That was how he remembered his predecessors doing it as "successful" businessmen. Being the boss meant not only holding to the letter of the law but also protecting the institution that had put him where he was. He had lost his "human" side years ago, so there was no longer anything to guard or hide.

For a while, Eli was able to live the divided existence—warm at home, cold at work. Inch by inch his cold exterior bled over into the small pool of home warmth he allowed himself. In neglecting to bring his warmth and flexibility to the workplace, he cheated his employees out of his most authentic self. Day by day he destroyed his spirit.

Divided We Fall

Compartmentalization is not compatible with spiritual leadership. When we fragment and cut off any portion of our life it tends to lose its vitality. When we show only the parts of ourselves we want others to see, we withhold a part of our essence.

Take the example of two physicians: One doctor responds stoically to her patients' concerns, always wears a neatly pressed lab coat, and knows every hospital regulation by heart. The other doctor takes time to be sure his patients are comfortable, listened to, and informed. He doesn't mind being rumpled by a friendly hug and bends the rules if it means everyone is going to be a little happier. Both physicians do the same job, both make about the same amount of income, yet their daily conduct is as different as night and day.

The point is that your leadership, whether the CEO of a major corporation or the owner of the local hot dog stand, provides you with an enormous amount of leeway. The choice is yours whether you take the freedom as a context for being more open and human or whether you mimic safe, restrictive expectations. Will you keep a soft schedule and remain people friendly, or will you try to fit one more task into your day? It is a personal decision unrelated to competence or duty or anything else you might use as an excuse. Will your rule be the clock on your wall or the care of your people?

The reality is that the more responsibility you have, the greater the possibility for freedom of self-expression. Let go of unnecessary rules. You have the opportunity to move beyond the rigidity and stereotypes into job excellence. When your spirit is freed to greater heights of spontaneous initiative, you can also free others who work with you to be their best creative selves.

The Unique Human Situation

Some bureaucrats and authority figures tend to enforce rules and regulations quite literally, as though the rules and regulations are the highest level of importance. They overlook the unique human situation where these rules are to be personally applied. This scenario seems to be a recurring theme in Maria's life. She has been that "unique human" involved. The political quickly becomes personal. Here is Anna Martinez's description:

The one button I still have that is easily pushed is the one called "You're really not doing your job competently." It usually occurs when "the boss" thinks I've stepped over some administrative line or bent some unwritten rule that threatens his authority. It often comes in the form of a memo. Some executives never deal directly with such matters. The edict is issued without shared process or explanation of how he arrived at the rule. That is, until I, ten drafts later, respond to his memo.

Somehow, he is always surprised that I respond. Then it seems to turn into a win/lose situation. My memo is, of course, answered with a third memo from him. It usually states: (1) how stupid I am to take this so personally, (2) that he only did it for my own good and the good of the company, (3) that it's due to insurance regulations or the vote of some nebulous body, and (4) it is completely out of his control. He was just doing his job. I COULD JUST SCREAM!!!

Brush it off and keep going, I tell myself. Instead, it is times like these when I feel most vulnerable. The weight of judgment is upon me. Shutting down, I begin to pull away from relationships. I don't want to deal with this. I'll just do my job—sitting silently at meetings, weighing sentences carefully, and measuring reactions with calculation—all for survival. I no longer live freely. Charisma and creativity are bottled up along with my frustration and anger. I stop sharing the fullness of who I am because it seems not to be valued over the rules and regulations. I know I do an excellent job for those we serve. They constantly express their appreciation. But is it worth the aggravation, lack of support, and even harassment back at the home office?

When we get burned at work, like Anna our first reflex is to pull in our sails, lie low, play it safe. Work only the hours strictly necessary. They can do anything to us except stop the clock, we reason, as we read the personnel manual and stick to it letter by letter. We stop risking the creative self-expression that makes our work shine and brings dividends to the institution. Let's admit it: There is no quicker way to cripple and destroy an organization than to obey every single rule and regulation. We know that it takes only a few people doing exactly what they are supposed to do to halt the creative forward movement of an organization.

Have you ever been burned at work? Can you recall times when you got tired of fighting the battles and drew a line in the sand? Perhaps you made a pledge to yourself never to cross it. The last time you did, you were sorry. There is too much chance of being hurt again.

Indeed, there are times when it is helpful to withdraw and gather ourselves within. We give ourselves permission to step back and lick our wounds. We spend time with intimate friends. We try to preserve ourselves and our souls. We can put up with any situation for a time, but living under a cloud day after day and year after year spells destruction. It diminishes our spirit, making us grow either numb or angry. Becoming indifferent and distant from our families, we no longer remember how to be open and carefree. We become out of touch even with ourselves as integrated persons: spirit, heart, and soul.

Compartmentalization is unspiritual. It is divisive in all parts of life, because it does not relate life as a whole. Don't think that you can compartmentalize your life and remain a spiritually whole person. In truth, divided persons are dangerous individuals masquerading with phony personas. They are frauds who continually reap rewards from the systems that so painstakingly raised them.

The nightmare in all this is that each one of us could wake up to find we have become like Eli or Maria. Any business, institution, or corporation, whether staffed by paid employees or volunteers, is a hard place for you to work and keep your soul. If we are not spiritually integrated, it could happen. We stand on guard to ensure that our integrated spiritual selves illuminate our entire lives and that our spiritual essence informs all that we do. People who lead with the spirit fight against compartmentalizing and work to keep their lives and spirits one unified whole.

The Fabric of Integration

If you are not presently integrated, don't panic. You cannot wake up one day and say, "I think I'll be integrated today." Instead, you will need to deal with one facet of your life at a time. As we grew to adulthood we decided which parts of ourselves we would share and which parts we would withhold. As children, some of us learned to do this to survive. If this is your story, you did it to protect your soul from irreversible harm. This was fine. It served you then and carried you until today. Now your hard task is to weave each piece of your life back into the fabric of your soul.

Merge the roles of your life into one: employment and work, family, friends, and faith communities. This means the manager, the life partner, the administrator, and the caregiver will be patiently woven into one tapestry. Set aside time to work each separate thread. All are part of the whole. As this new self emerges, you become the person you were meant to be.

What Do Integrated Leaders Look Like?

What do integrated leaders look like? Integrated leaders use the same respectful tone at work that they use with their children. The economic strategies they employ to buy groceries are the same ones they use when purchasing office supplies. The safety concerns they hold for their children, who are entrusted to them by God, they hold for their factory workers as well. If they care for animals and don't use animal-tested products at home, they refrain from using animal-tested products at work. If they live like holy people for one hour on the Sabbath, then they live like holy people during their forty-hour work week. If they live in well-kept homes, they will not be slum landlords in others' neighborhoods.

We know the difference the woven threads of justice and mercy make in leaders. Spirit-led people are not divided or compartmentalized. They work to remain whole and true to God, themselves, and the people they lead.

Moving from Compartmentalization to Wholeness

So, how do we begin to integrate all of who we are into our daily lives? How do we stop our divided living patterns? It is easier to keep the parts of life in compartments than to deal with the hard Spiritwork of integration. To move from compartmentalization to wholeness means three things. First, you make a commitment to change. Second, you are willing to be transparent. Third, you are ready to admit and accept your own faults and imperfections.

1. Commitment to change

Honest, effective leaders emerge only through real self-reflection, personal honesty, and a commitment to change. We work to be "honest to God." We walk in a different light, holding up the mirror so we can see ourselves as God does.

Let's admit it; commitment is not a popular notion, because commitment costs. What does it cost? It costs honesty. To be spiritually centered persons, we must be committed to being forthright and honest, first with ourselves and then with other people. This means being vulnerable enough for others to see our complete lives—the good, the bad, and the ugly. We live and project only who we authentically are. We are faithful to change throughout our lifetimes.

The integrated leader also believes that other people can change. No one's personality is set in stone. Instead, other people, like us, are constantly changing from who they are to who they are becoming. With this understanding, we are nonjudgmental and keep communication lines open. We are careful not to box people in and throw away the key as if there were no way the Spirit could work in their lives. We remain open to see and expect growth within them, just as we expect it in ourselves.

In committing to change, it is important to see ourselves for who we are. This means doing the hard work of self-examination. As you prod and probe in your examination, you cannot rush the answers. Sometimes you may need to sit with your questions in silence and prayer. You may need to carry them around with you for a time. Reflecting with a trusted friend is always helpful.

2. Willingness to be transparent

When we try to be who we are not, we get in trouble. To live a lie is to always be looking over your shoulder, living on the edge. When we are dishonest we haunt our souls, possessed by the power of the lie we are living. We become defensive and cannot be our own best selves.

Outward and inward honesty are what we strive for as leaders. We commit to being transparent. We project to others none other than our authentic self. We do not have hidden parts of our lives that cannot be shown. There is not a secret life behind the persona we project. Another way to put it is, "What you see is what you get."

Of course, when we open ourselves in this way we can expect hurt. Attorney General Janet Reno, living with the constant onslaught of criticism after the fiery death of David Koresh and his followers at Waco in 1993, said, "Hurt is a crucible. I came back stronger, and now the people who hurt me are my friends."

3. Admitting and accepting faults

Persons who lead are always committed to the openness of admitting and accepting their faults. If they do something wrong, they face it. This gives courage and confidence the next time. They know they are not perfect and are forever being perfected. Leaders admit when they are wrong and move quickly to acknowledge their mistake. They reconcile it as best they can.

Take James, for example. While on the job he missed apprising a co-worker about an important scheduled meeting. He thought he had sent a notice to everyone, but overlooked informing one of the most important managers. "At first I wanted to blame everyone else for my mistake, including my secretary. But when I took full responsibility for what I'd done, the power to reconcile it came back to me. It felt clean to simply call, explain, and offer my apology." James knew he had made the better move. In religious circles, this is called confession. James was willing to confess his own brokenness and ask for forgiveness. His act showed respect for the other person. Through confession, and then forgiveness, a new integration of spirit and body is made possible.

93

The "I want it all" Syndrome

"I want it all," Jacque said to her trusted friend Jeff. "I aim to do it all and have it all." In a flurry, Jacque shared her "all" philosophy of life with him. "I plan to see the world and raise my preschooler. I dream of a solid marriage and all the adventures of the single life. I want to be everything to everyone—a good mother, loving wife, competent executive, attentive daughter, creative writer, vivacious speaker, and leader—par excellence!" Her list went on. Why not? Wasn't it possible?

Jacque sat, smugly waiting for Jeff's admiration. Instead, there was a deafening pause. When Jeff's silence finally got Jacque's attention, he said, "Jacque, you think you want it all because you can't decide what you want. I think it's time to make some decisions before you wake up to find yourself scattered and nowhere." Jacque knew Jeff spoke the truth. What she thought was high-level enthusiasm was really indecision and lack of commitment.

Jeff went on to share his own story, which included an affair that ended his marriage and full-time fatherhood to his six-year-old daughter. "I thought I wanted it all, too," Jeff said, remembering his own bad case of the "I want it all" syndrome. "In truth, there were decisions I refused to make that were eventually made for me. I wish I had appreciated what I had instead of thinking I had to have everything I thought I desired." Jeff still looks back, wondering how things could have been different.

Jacque was suffering from the "I want it all" syndrome before her wise friend introduced her to the new philosophy of "enough." Taking inventory, she saw that her life already held everything she needed for happiness. She simply had to make basic decisions before they were made for her. It's as a wise friend shared with me, "It's not having what you want in life that brings happiness. Instead, it's wanting (and valuing) what you have."

Evelyn Underhill, in her book *The Spiritual Life: Great Spiritual Truths for Everyday Life*, shares this wisdom, "We mostly spend [our] lives conjugating three verbs: to want, to have, and to do. Cravings, clutching and fussing, on the material, political, social, emotional, intellectual—even on the religious—plane, we are kept in perpetual unrest: forgetting that none of these verbs has any ultimate significance, except so far as they are transcended by, and included in, the fundamental verb, to be: and that being, not wanting, having and doing, is the essence of the spiritual life."

Living the Present Moment *Now*

Do you suffer from the "I want it all" syndrome? Does contentment elude you? Do you fear you might suddenly wake up to see that you missed what was most important? Sadly, there is no going back. Lost years cannot be reclaimed. Your choice is to begin living the present moment—*now*. Adopting a new philosophy of enough means beginning to live in the present moment. When you live in the present moment, right now, you begin to see life differently. You view your desires, cravings, and efforts from a widened horizon. You acknowledge the long-denied deep spiritual influences in your life. As you take seriously this divine presence in your life, you find release and contentment. You reassess what is important and gives your life meaning and direction. As you recognize yourself as essentially a spiritual creature, you begin to live life to its fullest and most creative end.

My advice for getting through the tough times?

- Feed the kids, the cats, and the turtles.
- Have fun.
- Be in tune with your heart's desire.
- Don't be like Eli.
- Weave integration into your life.
- Live in the *enough* of the present moment.

And get out of bed and get to work.

To Thine Own Self Be True

Spiritwork: Reaching intimacy

The capacity for intimacy is a mark of mature leadership. Real leaders need real intimacy. The capacity for intimacy, which I define as the ability to deeply connect with others as well as wholly with oneself, is a mark of maturity. It involves being in touch with one's own depths and accepting one's feelings. Intimate persons yearn for real living and real connections with persons who value and affirm them. The intimate person is able to share himself or herself with another.

Some people are not able to be intimate. Their lives are directed by extrinsic values only, rather than internal needs. They gain their identity through conforming to the needs of a structure or system outside themselves. Because they deny their feelings, their emotional selves are not available—not even to themselves. Therefore, these persons cannot share with others what they don't have. Cursory relationships don't give them the personal support they need. Because they don't relate to others at much more than a surface level, they live in fearful vigilance and

constraint and are incapable of nonrationalized spontaneity. By repressing their emotional selves, sadly, the mystery of intimacy is closed to them.

Intimate companionship is essential if you are to continue to lead from light and not darkness. As you learn to
trust your abilities to discern your own feelings, wants,
and needs and to name what is ultimately life-giving for
you, you will learn to appreciate and respect the same
process in others.

There are a number of things you'll want to know about
yourself before you can share them and be intimate with
another. These "things" are the essence of what this book
is about. Basics include knowing who you are and what is
essential to you. Being aware of inner preferences and the
values you hold dear are also important. You'll want to
know what you want and need as well as what you think
and feel. In these defined ways, you are intimate with
yourself before you can be intimate with others. Ann
Wilson Shaef, in her book *Escape from Intimacy*, suggests
that "intimacy is being present to oneself and then being
able to bring that self to another." Nicely put.

Intimacy is:

• listening to another person in ways that are not judg-
mental or an offering of advice;
• talk that comes from the seldom-reached abyss of our
being;
• sensual, but not necessarily sexual or romantic;
• complementary and affirming;
• walking with another with eyes fully open and being fully
alive;
• experiencing life together, creating a common history and
connection;
• spaciousness, knowing when to be apart, and togetherness;
• safe space to make foolish mistakes or to cry, to play, and
to have fun;
• created from within, not with gimmicks or techniques;
• relationships that do not value others less;

• hard work, something worth laboring for;
• a mystery of the divine presence beyond understanding;
• a gift—always.

Not all of these attributes are found in every intimate relationship. One understanding holds firm: Intimacy is caring for yourself and then sharing that care with another.

The Need for Intimacy

Most of the chapters in this book have been written with relative ease. To struggle with the subject of intimacy is quite a different matter. It feels threatening. It is a complex issue central to our happiness or unhappiness. Our own deepest feelings are written in the margins of each page. There are no simple answers. Instead, what we offer to the conversation are parts of our personal lover's quarrel with intimacy, coupled with sex and sensuality, in relationships at work and at home. The struggle for intimacy with friends, long-term companions, children, parents or spouse, sexual partners, neighbors, and our faith community continues for as long as we live. Openness is required to begin again, unlearning old behaviors ingrained since childhood. This is a monumental task but a necessary one for those of us who want to lead from a spiritual center.

Leaders need intimacy. Leaders cannot survive long without companions who nurture the soul, some short-term and casual, others intense, close, and long-term. We need relationships, kinships, and friendships on a variety of levels. Our inner circle of companionship needs to be fine-tuned so we can function in healthy ways with those in our wider circle of responsibility.

We live out our intimacy needs in multifaceted ways. Intimacy levels vary with time, opportunity, and life circumstances. In companionship, we move through births, deaths, marriages, divorces, difficulties with children, and retirement. Most of our closest relationships are formed outside of the workplace. Family is often primary.

A certain level of intimacy may be developed with people at work or in your organization. A few close friendships may even be developed with colleagues. We spend a substantial number of hours with these people at work. This may mean sharing moments and experiences, or simply being present with one another. We build collegiality while telling a humorous story over coffee or lamenting over work schedules.

We cannot relate to all people in the same intimate way. Our communion of intimacy with others, at all levels, is a celebration of life, lifting our spirits and making our days lighter. All of these persons are our companions throughout life's journey.

A Fragile Weaving

Intimacy is a fragile weaving of togetherness and spaciousness. Both are needed and necessary. To be known and to know others is intricate to the weaving of intimacy. Relationships in which you share a good joke or act like a buffoon, dance until midnight or cry until daybreak are all part of the fabric. You find people you can lean on and others who depend on you. Hopefully, you have friends to whom you pour out your heart, but silences are okay too. You may have a partner who satisfies sexual needs and understands when you would rather not.

Sometimes in the search to fill our loneliness we are disappointed with our partner, children, parents, siblings, co-workers and friends. We long for the openness that could be ours. Anticipating relationships that nourish our spirits, we are drawn into the promise rather than the reality. Many times we are disappointed, for these persons cannot offer us what they do not themselves possess. They are incapable of intimacy because, estranged from their internal information system, they have no access to themselves. Therefore, they have nothing to offer us. We take our pulse, praying the same is not true for us.

Leaders often possess the very traits that result in isolation: the need to conform to company norms and to play out rigidly defined roles, and the drive for perfection—

the need to prove yourself invincible. People who are resistant to intimacy most likely attract the very friends and business associates who themselves hide from intimacy. So instead of working for true intimacy, they fake it with stand-away hugs, pats on the back, and air kisses. They may even share secrets with strangers. They may fool themselves with substitutes for the real thing for a while, but still the storm of need continues to rage within.

We want to be open, to know our own inner feelings, and to acknowledge our deepest desires. We want to let go of the ingrained patterns, preconceived notions, and drives that bind our spirits. We crave the joy of such freedom! But instead of undertaking the hard work that such intimacy requires, we often choose to remain with what we know. It feels safer to stay with what is familiar. In the end, estrangement is maintained.

I invite you to pause and take an inventory of your relationships.

With whom can you safely risk being spontaneous and open?

With whom can you reveal your true feelings and intentions?

Make a list of these persons so you will know where to start. Intentionally schedule time to meet for conversation with one or two of them. Start small by revealing a not-so-significant personal problem with which you are struggling. This might concern your decision to join an exercise class or your impending move to a new apartment. Unless you first talk about the "trivial" things in life you will never trust the relationship or yourself enough to share the big traumas and issues that arise.

Role Playing Destroys Intimacy

In the song "Eleanor Rigby," the Beatles asked, "All the lonely people, where do they all come from?"

There are a lot of lonely people out there. You may be one of them. Joyce was. Following the death of her husband, she became obsessed with living out her expected role of grieving wife.

"I was so concerned about pleasing everyone else that I lost who I was. I was less than genuine even to myself and yet the outward appearance was as if all were well. I thought that others would love me more for behaving in a certain way. I frequently substituted one close relationship for another when I felt someone was getting too close. I hid behind a rigid image of my role as the weeping widow. In reality, my husband had been sick for so long that it was a relief when he died. I felt freer and more lighthearted than I had for years."

Joyce's persona of superficial pretenses may have projected a normal personality, but not necessarily a spiritually centered one. What she was unaware of at the time was the way such manipulations backfire over the long run. In Joyce's case, it pushed the people she wanted to have closest further and further away.

What intimacy and warmth I did experience during this time usually came unexpectedly. These moments appeared without schedule or warning. They came when I had my guard down and did not control or plan the happening, such as when a surprise party was given in my honor or when I became ill and had to be cared for. I now thank God for these grace-filled moments that offered me a fleeting glimpse of what a full life in intimate relationship could be.

I was in graduate school during the time that I became more and more withdrawn from the people around me. In my loneliness, and by this time depression, I sought professional counseling. Thank God! The counselor listened for long hours, helping me to make sense of my story. Then one day, looking me squarely in the eye, the counselor said, "I think you now know the price is too high to continue wearing your mask. If you want to break out of this loneliness, you are going to have to take it off."

Joyce learned that role playing is a chief destroyer of intimacy. Her life had become too unbearable. The cost of hiding her true self behind an elaborate facade of superficial pretenses was too high. She knew she either had to risk sinking further into depression or surrender the role. Joyce found the recovery process slow and painful. "Inch by inch I intentionally opened myself to certain persons. I shared small matters first and gradually worked my way up to revealing personal information about my true feelings, fears, and dreams. I had to be willing to be embarrassed with friends. Two of these friends remain my closest companions even today. They know my history and all of who I am and accept me, lock, stock, and barrel."

Most of us have pretty good intuitions about who we can trust, with whom we can and cannot be intimate. Most times, when we have been hurt, we look back and realize we sensed it was not a good idea from the beginning. Opening ourselves to others is risky, but as we stop playing roles, we take small steps toward intimacy. We discover that the person we tried to hide is really the polestar that attracts the love and support we desire.

Conversations of the Heart:
Hearing Each Other to Speech

To keep a healthy spirit, you need to have conversations that are close and up front. True conversation is centered not only in words, but also in listening to the heart of another. It is not talk filled with technical methodology or intellectual information. Instead, it contains metaphoric images and authentic reflections. In *The Intimate Connection*, James B. Nelson writes, "We are yearning for closer, more fulfilling, more life-giving connections with others, with our world and with ourselves. This means we are yearning for closer connectedness with God, the heart of the universe itself. Another way of saying this is that we are simply longing for more life-giving connections between our sexuality and our spirituality."

Let's not fool ourselves. We don't establish intimacy by pouring out our entire life story to anyone who will listen. Disclosure of this proportion may in fact hinder the building of an intimate companionship. Intimacy is not necessarily established by spending more time with people. Instead, intimacy is accomplished a bit at a time as your spirit intermingles with and engages another. In places of work, this can mean talking over project details or sharing everyday concerns. Intimacy is broached when two souls meet and experience a new speech, perhaps haltingly at first. It is an intimacy that comes only with hearing the spirit.

We all have had times when we immediately experienced the powerful feeling of connectedness with another person. The "Ah-ha" moment passes over us like a wave. Haven't you conversed with someone in a normal pattern and suddenly heard yourself expressing feelings you had not beforehand realized were inside? Thoughts and memories long suppressed and stored away came surging out. Feelings you didn't know existed were called out by this one now listening.

Understanding Different Forms of Communication

Talk is one tool we use at work to build relationship. We can also use it to block relationship. Different people view conversations in different lights. Some people view talk as a way of creating intimacy, connecting to another. For example, George may stop his task and ask for directions, seeing it as an opportunity for a fleeting connection with a co-worker. Kim Lee shares a work problem with a colleague and feels better about it because she feels connected.

Other people view talking as a way to negotiate status; it establishes "one-up" or "one-down" standing. Unlike George and Kim Lee, Bernice feels that in asking for directions she is admitting her ignorance, diminishing her to a "one-down" position. Anthony, in sharing his job-related difficulties with an associate, thinks he only wallows in his own misery and feels even worse. Spirit-centered leaders can find themselves trapped in a "catch-22."

In a meeting, Jina, the supervisor-in-charge, asks for feedback from co-workers about a particular problem facing the department. Jina openly expresses her concern and uncertainly about changes that need to be made. She is a spiritually centered leader who believes in sharing the decision-making processes with those closest to the problem. John, who works for her, does not see it this way. He views Jina's sharing as a signal that she doesn't know what she's doing. He expects his boss to be "in control" at all times or to assume control at a moment's notice. He views Jina's open supervisory process as a show of weakness, and he responds by questioning her competence and wellness instead of recognizing it as the strength and wisdom that it is.

Some of these variations can be attributed to gender differences. Others are due to innumerable social and psychological reasons. Deborah Tannen, in her best-selling book on male-female communications, *You Just Don't Understand: Women and Men in Conversation*, warns that the risk involved in ignoring sex differences in the workplace is greater than the danger in naming them. In an interview, she shared a word of advice, "If women can begin to understand that intimate talk doesn't have the same meaning to a man as it does to them—and men can begin to understand women need to share and connect—then maybe at least people can avoid the feeling that something is terribly wrong with their relationship. Realizing that a partner's behavior is not his or her individual failing, but a normal expression of gender lifts this burden of blame and disappointment. Understanding gender differences in ways of communication is the first step toward change."

Female or male, we have the power to hear one another in ways that nourish and heal. In our institutions, organizations, and churches we need a freeing word that expresses the new spiritual reality. It is a word powerful enough to make a difference in us and in the lives of those around us. Nelle Morton, in her book *The Journey Is Home*, contemplates, "Perhaps there is a word that has not yet come to sound—a word that once we begin to speak will round out and create deeper experiences for us and put us in touch with sources of power, energy of which we are just beginning to be aware." Morton talks about her own experience, which she creatively labeled "hearing other persons to speech." She states that this intimate speech is "organic because it comes up out of the deepest abyss of our being. We were drawn into one another's presence. We began hearing one another to speech. We experience God, as Spirit, hearing human beings to speech—to new creation." Many of us, like Morton, are not in touch with our own feelings until we sort out the story with someone willing to actively listen.

Morton asks, "Is it that we await a new word that we cannot yet speak?" Our vocabulary is so limited. We know that we are affected by the language (or lack thereof) we use. Entering the search, we find new words in leadership to express what is struggling to be born. We need new imagery to live our spiritual life in its fullness and enable others to do the same. Spirit-centered leaders seek to harmonize relationships. Alliances that have been torn apart by inadequate or hurtful language, depriving the working woman or man of humanness, are brought to wholeness again.

From Communication to Relationship

I recently served as a study leader at a three-day spiritual conference. The subject was advocacy for children, a conversation overdue in a country where a large number of children continue to wake up hungry, abused, and unloved. In a short time the participants not only dealt with the emotional heaviness the statistics required, but they also laughed and played through children's games, blowing giant bubbles, and learning to circle dance. The participants caught the childlike spirit of freedom. Childhood memories arose out of the experience as they listened to each other's story in small sharing groups, over meals, and during breaks.

Birdella whispered her story of fifteen years of sexual abuse. Russell, a ninety-year-old, shared his sense of abandonment as friends and family died, leaving him behind. Bonnie arrived late to the second session tightly clutching a big furry teddy bear. I didn't ask why. Later she told of the one hundred extra pounds of weight she once carried as her emotional insulation. Clare, an expert on everything, never talked about her personal life. But we sensed her captivity and rejoiced when once, with abandonment, she laughed with us.

For a few fleeting hours, these women and men allowed themselves to touch the oozing sores and spirited pleasures of childhood. The silence, once stifled, now yielded its own story. The group listened in heartfelt ways that brought Birdella and Russell, Bonnie and Clare to speech. Each person left a bit more hopeful and in touch with his or her child-spirit. They experienced the affirming touch of intimacy. And they were better prepared to be effective leaders in their advocacy for children.

Community is built one relationship at a time. One by one we build this connection. The Divine's will for our lives cannot be discovered in isolation. We find God's purpose as we interact with the people around us. We pay attention to needs and give energy to desires to find a self-unfolding and growth. Living out of our true calling, we enable others to do the same.

• We develop and care for relationships that feed our deepest needs for intimacy.
• We intentionally create opportunities where we listen to others and are listened to in ways that nurture the spirit.
• We seek safe space to speak the truth, to name what is false, and to know we are not crazy in systems that are insane.

Six Practical Suggestions for Intimacy

Beginning today, look for opportunities to give of yourself and to receive what others share. Set aside time to be with your family, friends, and faith community. You have a primary responsibility to yourself and to the people you care about. Spend time in their presence and share yourself with them. Here are six other practical suggestions for your new life of intimacy.

1. *Choose friends who are good to you and to themselves.* They should be persons who feel good about themselves and about you. Hanging out with them, you gain a clearer understanding of the healthy, happy person you are meant to be. Seek out people who support your growth just as you make every effort to support them. You need people who are healthy and balanced. Together you will nurture one another. Fill your world with people who have a purposeful attitude and a caring respect for themselves and others. Don't settle for less!

2. *Check yourself if you find you are gravitating toward people who are unbalanced, unhappy, and disrespectful.* Getting bogged down in unstable relationships takes too much energy that can be used in more creative ways. If you sense you are being pulled toward self-defeating relationships, recognize them and pull back. Refuse to cultivate the insanity that comes from living with abusive people. You do not have to be physically or emotionally abused. Don't enter into crazy relationships and then wait for the destruction to end.

3. *Realize that some people simply are incapable of the care and approval you require.* Liberate yourself and accept the reality that some people have a very limited capacity for relationship and intimacy. Let go of the anger and resentment you have felt and accept them for who they really are (or were). As one esteemed friend, Adele Wilcox, writes in her book *Self and Soul,* "You can't get out of people what they can't give." Do not expect friends, family members, or work associates to offer a level of intimacy beyond their capabilities. You will be more content and happier in all of your varied relationships.

4. *Choose to see the limits of relationships.* Enter into relationships knowing that no one can care for all of your needs. We expect relationships to sweep away our low self-esteem, to give us new purpose in life, and to heal all of our childhood wounds. We search for the perfect friend who will always understand, always be available, and never disappoint us. No human being can live up to such expectations, so don't expect them to.

5. *Enter into relationships with respect for your own individuality.* Trust yourself to receive care and handle hurt; receive loyalty and deal with betrayal. Respect the other person as he or she is, and expect this person to respect you. Do not melt into that person, losing your own identity. Neither expect this person to deny who he or she is and become like you. Instead, join in partnership to complement and support each other. Do not give up your individuality but use who you are as a whole person to enhance the relationship.

6. *Trust your intuition when dealing with other people.* Listen to what your inner voice tells you about people. Acknowledge what you admire or dislike in others and recognize what is admirable in yourself and what you might change. Know that you can show anger and still care for others. Take other people's anger as information and the opportunity to build the relationship rather than as rejection. Stay away from self-defeating behaviors in your relationships.

The Choice for Intimacy Is Yours

Are you ready to make the necessary changes to create and sustain healthy intimate relationships? Here are five questions to ask yourself.

1. Are you taking the time to sort out relationships with a new awareness?

2. Do you believe that you deserve relationships with family, friends, colleagues, and associates that are healthy and sustainable?

3. Will you work with your relationships to their fullest realistic potential?

4. What roadblocks separate you from intimate relationships?

5. Can you recognize the barriers and work in honesty with yourself and the other person to alleviate any barriers that falsely divide you?

My hope is that you will, through intentional choices, be better equipped to live in intimacy, that you will have a deepened self-awareness that leads to relationships that are healthy and whole. Spirit-centered leaders not only have the wish to know another's inner life but also build the ability to share their own. When we have primary relationships that meet our intimacy needs, we are happier and more contented leaders in our places of work and service.

I pray you will no longer deceive yourself by entering into harmful relationships that cannot fulfill your real needs. It takes hard work for some of us to discover our needs and inner feelings. It takes understanding our pasts and reckoning with our present circumstances. And then, when they are available, we must be ready to speak these thoughts to another. Only then are we ready to accept the challenge and do the work that leads to true intimacy.

Sex and Soul

Spiritwork: Connecting body
and spirit

God has so extravagantly given us the gift of sexuality. Leaders can use this gift in ways that honor and care for others. We can act in ways that respect and reverence others. Our sense of sexuality centers on "whole-personed" intimacy and accepts each expression of care as an end unto itself. Expressions of this kind of beauty are essential to our wholeness and well-being. The effects of such care are stunning. As we grow to know ourselves, we come to accept and appreciate the wonders of all the sensual-sexual characteristics within ourselves, both masculine and feminine.

Sexuality and Sensuality at "One"

It is absolutely essential that leaders deal with their sexuality. Let's begin the examination by asking, "How do you experience your sexuality? Do you experience it trustingly and responsibly?" It is important to explore the intrinsic linking of sexuality and spirituality, to understand how you bring sexuality into your work relationships. Your sexuality is a key part of your whole self as a human being. We are not physically, sexually involved with most of the people we care about in our life spans. But with some we are. Yet, sexuality plays a primary role in all of our relationships. How can we understand sexuality better and enjoy it more? How can we change attitudes that keep us from freely enjoying sexuality within ourselves and others?

To be at one with ourselves physically, emotionally, and spiritually and to be at peace with one another is the goal of our sexual and personal wholeness. The term *sex* or *sexual* is not understood within our culture in the best of ways. To be a sexual person is often to be objectified by society. Perhaps the term *sensual* or *sensuality* would read more holistically. *Sensual* defines more clearly who we are as spiritual and sexual beings. When our sexual person and our spiritual person are in harmony and at one with each other, we experience our sensual selves in such simple pleasures as hugging a friend, walking on a warm spring day, holding a baby, or tasting the first strawberries of the season.

Experiencing the Divine

Let's examine those relationships in which we are sexual in a physical way. These would not be the people at work, unless we are in business with our life-mate. We sense we are sitting in the center of the holy when we are in the midst of our sexuality. Sexuality is experiencing the divine in other persons as they pour themselves into our lives. There is nothing as freeing and joyous as a loving, committed sexual relationship. It is a profoundly satisfying pleasure of life.

Sexual relationships can be intense. They puzzle, frustrate, energize, potentially oppress, and hopefully free us. They enable us to learn more about ourselves and our lovers and to get close in ways we never expected. They raise issues of power and vulnerability, commitment and risk. Sexual relationships can be painful, such as when a longtime union dissolves. A love affair promises much and then fizzles. A lover dies. A marriage turns abusive. Most of us want and need intimacy, so we usually recover from the hurt and try again.

Penelope Washburn, author of *Becoming Woman*, helps readers to focus understanding of the complexities of sexuality and spirituality. Washburn shares that to enter into the physical sharing act of love to a person, when love and trust are not involved, carries deep pain and emotional cost. Persons feel divided and split in two by discordant feelings and actions. To "make love" to a person you do not love is a form of spiritual death. It feels fundamentally self-deceptive. The experience of sex is not only a matter of trusting the other person but of trusting yourself and your sexuality. To be one, physically and emotionally, with yourself and with the other person is a goal of sexual satisfaction and spiritual wholeness.

Sex and Intimacy

There has been a continuing unhealthy split between our sexuality and intimacy. We have failed to fully integrate sexuality and spirituality, body and soul, sensuality and friendship. This failure sets up the opposite sex to be objectified as "sex objects." The act of sex, as in sexual relationship with another, is not necessarily intimacy, although it is one way we reach for intimacy. Sex may be connected to intimacy—may even sometimes be the result of it.

This is an intricate facet of relationships that leaders cannot ignore. Our hormones, if nothing else, will not let us! We are flattered by persons who are drawn to us. Leaders find themselves with followers who idolize them. People give us a place of authority in their lives. Their need to please the leader makes them vulnerable and open. This giving over of power may be acted out in a number of ways, including sexual ways. This is called transference.

Flattery is very seductive. You get a taste of being adored and need to guard against being drawn into the lie. It does not matter if the other person seduces you, that you are both single, that his wife does not understand him or that she needed comforting. *There is never a good enough reason to take advantage of your leadership position and use another person sexually.*

Take care that you do not fabricate sophisticated explanations for the misuse of your power. Responsible leaders are always aware of "one up" and "one down" positions of power. "One up" and "one down" refer to wages, positions of seniority, or responsibilities that carry authority over other people. A leader never uses this leverage to take advantage of another person. You as the leader, as the person in power, are always ultimately responsible. To cross over the line and act out the encounter with sex is to take advantage of your position, betraying the relationship.

This is why Spirit-filled leaders have the responsibility to deal with their own sexuality. They lead in ways that are faithful to their position and do not violate the trust of those they are called to serve. Leaders are careful not to fool themselves with fabricated excuses for sexual encounters. Two books by Marie Fortune are worth your time. *Is Nothing Sacred?* specifically deals with sexual misconduct by people in power. A second, *Love Does No Harm,* is about the misuse of sex in relationships. I won't tell you that I "enjoyed" either book, but they did open my eyes.

The Crisis of Sex: Trust

The spiritual crisis of sex can be focused on one word: *trust.* Trust involves overcoming fears and taking responsibility for our sexuality. There are times when sexuality is viewed as the enemy. We experience our body as being divided from itself.

The crisis in our sexual experience is in being trusting, open, and vulnerable. When what is offered is given in trust and commitment to the other person, as in the covenant of marriage, then the experience of sex becomes graceful. Something more is given and received through the physical and emotional union of two persons than either person alone gives. Washburn, in *Becoming Woman*, states: "The emotional and spiritual impact of it transcends the actual experience; it brings peace, a feeling of oneness in the self and with the other, and a new self trust and mutuality."

Total union with our lover in that moment has been one of the best teachers of what is called grace. We become a new creation as we abandon ourselves to the totality of our mutual sexual interaction. We are, in that moment, both fully giving and fully receiving. We experience the grace and power of renewal through the totality of the mutual encounter. The emotional and spiritual impact transcends the actual experience. It brings peace, a feeling of oneness in the self and with the other, and a new self-trust and mutuality. The possibility of experiencing sex as a "graceful" encounter beckons us ever toward it.

Your body and spirit are not two separate entities, to be divided one from the other. Spirituality is both earthly and bodily. "You know that your body is a temple of the Holy Spirit, [who] is within—the spirit you [have] received from God—therefore glorify God in your body," to quote holy Scripture.

Our goal is to be better equipped to live our sexuality in intimacy with another person, to have a deepened self-awareness that leads to a relationship that is healthy and whole. We will then no longer deceive ourselves by entering into harmful relationships that cannot fulfill our real needs. With a greater sense of our needs and an understanding of our past, we are ready to accept the challenges of our sexuality and spirituality.

A Model to Follow

The story of the woman who broke into a banquet to anoint a man holds all the elements to demonstrate leaders' using their sexuality in ways that honor and care for other persons. Let me briefly share this ancient story as I gleaned it from Helen Bruch Pearson in her book *Do What You Have the Power to Do?* One day the Great Teacher, Jesus, was sitting at the table at a friend's house when a woman came in carrying an alabaster jar full of costly oil. Unexpectedly, she broke open the jar and poured it upon the Teacher's head. Standing at his feet, weeping, she began to bathe his feet with her tears and dry them with her hair. Then, kissing his feet, she anointed them with the oil and wiped them with her hair. The house filled with the oil's aroma.

This woman was as bold and unashamed as she was tender and compassionate. Pouring this lavish amount of precious oil over her beloved was an act so extravagant that it shocked the men in the room. They called her action into question, supposedly for being so wasteful. Yet, in truth, they knew that this woman did what they would not do. By her actions, she was touching, giving, anointing, and risking. In her silent act, she gave the intimate gift of her sensuality, offered with profound respect and reverence.

We can imagine that the Teacher, Jesus, longed for the tender act of love extended by this woman. He graciously received this woman's gift of presence. To be cared for and loved by this woman was balm to his weary soul. It brought healing to his wounded spirit. To simply sit and be cared for and ministered to so completely felt good. Indeed, when he is questioned by the other men in the group he tells them, "Leave her alone! Why are you bothering her? She has done a fine and beautiful thing for me."

There is beauty in what the woman did. She sensed what was right and fitting. She moved to action. We know, from Jesus' response, that he was pleased. He was sensitive to her deepest expressions of self-giving and affirmed the beauty of her actions. He defended the place of sexuality in the spiritual life of persons. Jesus understood and accepted it with grace but did not act on it. He could accept her sensuality for the gift that it was. He didn't abuse the relationship by turning around and taking her to bed. This is a model for leadership.

Sexuality is sacred and essential to the wholly integrated human experience. Sexuality is an experience of God's grace and love. As we gain a deeper sense of the sacredness of our own sexuality and allow it to claim its rightful place in the flow of our lives, we find harmony and confidence to live life luminously. As the body, mind, and heart find unity we claim our power to cease behaviors that may cause harm in our own or other people's lives.

In *Nature, Man and Woman,* Alan Watts writes of such love and sensuality:

> Contemplative love, like contemplative meditation . . . has no specific aim; there is nothing particular that has to be made to happen. . . . In a relationship that has no goal other than itself, nothing is merely preliminary. One finds out what it can mean simply to look at the other person, to touch hands, or listen to the voice. . . . The psychic counterpart of this bodily and sensuous intimacy is a similar openness of attention to each other's thoughts, a form of communication which can be as sexually "charged" as physical contact. This is the feeling that one can express one's thoughts to the other just as they are, since there is not the slightest compulsion to assume a pretended character. This is perhaps the rarest and most difficult aspect of any human relationship. . . . Yet this is quite the most important part of a deep sexual relationship and it is in some way understood even when thoughts are left unsaid. . . To unveil the flow of thought can therefore be an even greater sexual intimacy than physical nakedness.

I invite you to find a comfortable spot, close your eyes, and take a few minutes to reflect on your sexuality. You may want to consider sharing your reactions with a friend or companion. How do you express this sensuality in your life? Have you learned to affirm who you are, male or female, and reject the distorted views of the past? Have you rejected the Hollywood image of the perfect body? Can you affirm your sexuality and the unique beauty it holds? Do you celebrate the sexual part of yourself as a whole person of God? Do you feel free to share spiritual kinship through your sexuality in appropriate ways with people, both male and female? Can you share your sexual/sensual self without the need to possess or "own" another?

How do you experience your sexuality right now? The power to express ourselves sexually extends from the day we are born until the day we die. In each stage of life, our sexuality changes. Sexual awareness ebbs and flows depending on our life situation. It is a life-long learning process.

The True Test of Leaders

It is in our primary relationships with our children, parents, and friends that we can learn how to live out our sexuality in healthy ways so we can be Spirit-filled leaders. Because our families are such a big part of our identities, there is no way we can separate our vocational lives from our family lives. Yet, some corporation executives and business managers live as if this is not the reality. Family care gets a low priority in the corporate demand for commitment and sacrifice. Persons in decision-making positions in our employment systems would find more spirit if they would take into account the welfare of their employees' family life as they make corporate decisions.

Taking care of our sexual-sensual-spiritual life, as it relates to our family, is of primary importance. Or as a friend of mine so bluntly put it: "Tend your own garden, and the one on the other side of the fence won't look so green." In this time of high stress, cut backs, and corporate competition, our family or primary support group may be the one stabilizing place to find rest and refreshment for the days ahead. Care for our family keeps the spiritual dimension of our life alive.

Tending Our Gardens: An Affirmation
of Celebration

So what is the final word on sex? There is none. Instead, we are left with the struggle of living in the in-between. We've named some truths about what it takes to live as a Spirit-filled leader. We desire to live out our sexuality responsibly and in respectful ways that do not betray our followers.

Here is an affirmation to use as you reimage your sexuality and tend your garden.

As I grow to understand myself as a holy person, I accept and appreciate the wonders of all my characteristics, both feminine and masculine. I affirm my sexuality as essential to my well-being. I reject distorted views of the past. I no longer accept old myths about sex and myself as a sexual person. I know that sex is not for one person to wield power over another. Neither is sex what validates me as a man or a woman. If I was taught that sex is dirty, I now know this is untrue. Instead, I equate sex with care, love, and respect. With a newly lighted spirit, I am in tune with my sexual feelings.

I no longer pretend my body does not exist. Sexuality is a part of who I am as a total person of the divine, and I affirm my sexuality and the unique beauty it holds. I celebrate myself as a sexual person. This celebration is a tribute to myself and to the persons with whom I have chosen to share my life.

My intimate friend was right. We need to tend our own gardens.

Help Wanted: Spiritual Mentors and Guides

Spiritwork: Seeking soulful souls

I t is our responsibility to intentionally seek out, lift up, and nurture Spirit-filled persons for leadership. This part of our task is clear and within the realm of "do-ability." Spirit-filled leaders are needed in our places of work, volunteer organizations, government ranks, and religious institutions. We need persons with a lighted spirit serving in fast-food management and as the president of our country. Here is a warning: *If we do not intentionally seek leaders with these attributes, persons who are led by the Spirit and know that they are, if we do not elect and call persons who have made the inner journey into the deep and have emerged into the light, then we may end up with leaders who are spiritless and who work in darkness.*

Stop right now and ask yourself: "Who are three persons I am mentoring for leadership?" Spirit-centered leaders are mentors, both formally and informally. The community that takes the time and energy to discern, name, and commission spiritual persons will produce leaders who are Spirit-centered. If we fail to do this we may find ourselves with individuals in leadership positions who speak or preach effectively but who place themselves at the front and center to the detriment of others. These individuals simply happen to be at the right place at the right time. We may luck out and hit gold, but, without intention, most likely we will not have the leaders we want or need. Instead, they will simply be the individuals who have risen, in whatever manner—good or ill—to the top. And the top is not always the cream. Indeed, it may be unwanted residue that will later sour the milk.

Real Leaders for Difficult Times

We seek leaders who are real. As they are lead by the Spirit, they keep community central. Spirit-grounded leaders evolve over the long term. Our leaders need to be willing to make the commitment and have the driving desire to walk in the Spirit. Other desirable attributes include:

• accepting the cost of leadership and expecting the journey to be difficult;
• knowing that other people have gifts in their own right and valuing and esteeming these persons as truly worthy of their time and involvement;
• seeing each individual as a person of sacred worth;
• not viewing yourself as more spiritual or better than others (seasoned in their walk on the spiritual path, leaders live out what has been entrusted to them);
• knowing that you are not perfect and, more times than not, choosing right over wrong, the spiritual over the temporal;
• not telling others how they should live, but through your own life modeling the way of the Spirit;
• being grounded in hope, love, and peace and demonstrating it as you live in a global perspective;

• being a person of vision and purpose who "hungers and thirsts for righteousness."

We cannot train would-be leaders in these attributes, but we can give opportunities for prospective leaders to stretch their horizons and try their wings. We need to search out spiritually centered leaders, wherever they are. When we finally look upon such persons, hopefully we gravitate toward them. We respect, affirm, and acknowledge their commitment. We ask them to be our guides and mentors. We make space for them to try their wings and let them share their dreams with us. We commission, hire, or elect them, not for particular privilege, but for discipline, service, and accountability. As we recognize them for who they are, call them out as guides, and affirm their gifts, we will have the persons we need to lead us into tomorrow.

Mentoring for Leadership

We have two responsibilities: (1) mentoring others and (2) finding our own mentor. We have an obligation to lift up, help shape, and encourage other would-be leaders as well as to find persons who will do this for us. How do we begin as a mentor, and what should we look for in someone who would mentor us? It may seem awkward at first to have a serious mentoring relationship. You, perhaps, have little self-confidence in establishing a good spiritual friend and feel great vulnerability in approaching such a connection. Such a person does not have to be more "advanced" than you—although this would be helpful—but sensitive, intuitively perceptive, and empathic enough to provide you with the support you need.

Listed here are ten practical guidelines for you to consider as you practice mentoring or being mentored. As you read this list, ask yourself these two questions: Who can be a mentor for me? Can I be a mentor for someone else?

1. *Mentors whet the appetite for the things of the Spirit.* They have a personal spiritual commitment and an active

discipline of meditation and reflection. The only authority they possess is the power of their own persons as vessels of the Divine who take seriously their relationship to God and to others. They are capable of noticing the movement of the Spirit and have the capacity to step aside and let the Spirit be at work.

2. *Mentors commit to maintaining the tension between the inward journey and the outward journey.* They listen and hear themselves so as to be attuned to and to hear the needs of others.

3. *Mentors have a deep yearning to have a conscious relationship with themselves, with other people, and with God.* They need to have the ability to connect with other people in intimate ways.

4. *Mentors push horizons both for themselves and for us to deliver us from false securities, safe opinions, and known ways.* They have a healthy desire to live more fully, with more honesty and health and less self-inflicted pain. This desire keeps them and you at the task of overcoming resistance to growth and change.

5. *Mentors are involved in some concrete intervention at a point of the world's needs.* They may work with the poor, for legislative reform, or with the elderly. They have a personal, hands-on commitment to demonstrate the ways of holiness.

6. *Mentors teach us reticence so that we do not burden those who do not hunger and, therefore, cannot receive.* From them we learn when not to "cast our pearls before swine."

7. *Mentors encourage.* They do not stress the negative or dark sides of experiences. Instead, they lift up the positive. Care and warmth are elicited from the conversations and remain long after you leave one another.

8. *Mentors are the midwife rather than the healer.* Traveling with us, they provide an environment for the birth and nourishment of a whole soul. They approach the task with reverence and humility, in the spirit of a companion rather than an authority. They pass on to us the lessons learned in their own valleys, not as experts but as fellow

122

travelers helping us read the maps, avoid dead ends, and watch out for potholes. They have some experience and sympathy with our path.

9. *Mentors understand confidentiality and respect privacy needs.*

10. *Mentors do not project their own needs or agenda on another person.* They do not have an expectation or anticipation of who a person should be or where a person should go.

Me, a Leader?

You may be reading this book because you would like to be a leader. Do you believe you have the spirit and gifts for the task? Have you sensed yourself "swinging out over the rim" and "stepping beyond the limits"? Do you have the vision of "leading people home"? If you surmise, not solely through your own intellect or self-centered ego, but through the wisdom and nurturing of your community that you may be a Spirit-filled leader with the necessary gifts, then it is your responsibility to authenticate it with your community. As risky as it feels—and is—it is your obligation to step to the center of the circle. In stepping out, you trust that if the calling is true *and the time is right,* you will be lifted up for the good of the community for a season to serve. If not, with spirit intact, you will graciously step aside.

I stress *if the time is right* because the truth is that your faith community, organization, or place of business may not be ready for your leadership. This is not a reflection on you. There may be two good choices for leadership, and you are not the choice. The organization may not be ready to take on a new type of leader. Or it could be the inability of the system to either recognize or empower its most healthy and gifted persons. If you are working in a hierarchical establishment and have little seniority, a male who does not fit the accepted cultural norm, or a female, you may be hitting dead ends. These dead ends include a wide spectrum of symptoms. Ignoring or belittling contributions, misinterpreting actions, or actual sabotage may be taking place. Colleagues with their eyes on the prize may view you as competition and a threat to their ambitions. You could be dealing with jealousy. The exercising of your gifts may provoke fear in others. Other peers may perceive a move toward your leadership as not politically expedient. They may feel they have more to gain by supporting the status quo leadership or remaining quiet instead of supporting you.

Elizabeth O'Connor, in her book, *Eighth Day of Creation,* says this of creative people: "Because the old and successful have kingdoms to think about they are in a position to be even more threatened by the emerging gifts of others. The more full a promise of life is the more it is apt to evoke uncomfortable responses in others. If a community is to exist at all, it must learn to deal openly and creatively with feelings of jealousy and envy. Envy is a symptom of lack of appreciation of our own uniqueness and self-worth."

There is little you can do to counteract other people's actions or influence their perceptions. Remember that you cannot be less of who you are because of who other people are. As O'Connor says, "We cannot protect ourselves or others from envy by pretending that we are not the possessors of gifts. As we find courage to confess our envy, so we must find courage to confess our gifts."

In times like these, it is important to have a mentor to turn to. Check out what is "you" and what is "them," what circumstances are internal and can be controlled and what are external and, therefore, beyond anything you can affect. A friend shared this holy word from the Hebrew Scriptures. I keep it in my journal to read from time to time: "Fear not, for I am in the place of God. As for you, you meant harm against me, but God meant it for good."

Whatever the outcome for the present, you do not need to fear. Instead, go to trusted friends and colleagues whom you perceive are also on the spiritual journey. Ask for their discerning powers, reflections, and prayers. Then hear, really hear, what they have to say. If you respond with a "no" to leading when you are called, you may be missing your chance to live out God's will and purpose for your life.

To say yes will be to follow the lead of the Divine and to contribute your very best.

Grace-Filled Leaders Are a Gift

We are drawn to leaders who possess charisma. These are persons who have a personal charm that arouses our loyalty and enthusiasm. The Greek word *charismata* means "gift of grace." Persons with healthy charisma are a gift of grace to everyone they encounter. Through their work, the Spirit builds and informs, giving the community clearer vision. The gift also uplifts and enlightens the person who has it. There is a humble spirit that emerges as the leader sees how his or her words and actions affect the community. This person knows that he or she is not the motivater and worker of the good that emerges. Instead, leaders recognize that it is the Divine Spirit that lives and breathes within them. Their actions have a way of calling out the best in others as they are having the time of their lives doing what they are called to do. They recognize the divinity that resides in each person they meet, encouraging and enabling them to grow to become the fullest they can be.

Barbara is just such an example of healthy charisma.

Barbara, known for her sharp wit and ability to think on her feet, was invited to serve as the moderator of a professional panel discussion at the annual meeting. She was asked because she was a leader who had a personality that shined even on the dreariest of days. Barbara knew the importance of this opportunity. Many members of the Board of Directors would be present.

Checking first to get the go ahead, she created a dynamic duo. She sought out Megan, a new associate in the company. After extensive briefing, both Barbara and Megan shared the spotlight to moderate. By playing off each other, presenting differing views, they found that the panel time moved at an interesting, brisk pace in the midst of a long day of formal presentations. Barbara creatively used the opportunity to introduce her colleagues to another leader for the organization. In giving Megan the experience, Barbara empowered her with further self-confidence and experience for the younger associate's future work. Barbara was a role model who used her charisma for the good of the organization and the building up of her colleague.

Here is a second example of healthy charismatic leadership.

Jim was the presenter for a national seminar on stress management. He had attended many conferences in the past in which a sole presenter used a clip-on mike, slick media, and graphics to make a point. Participants sat in rows, behind writing tables, facing forward. At all times the attention of the audience was centered on the presenter. The person, front and center, was the star.

Jim decided to experiment with a new style of presentation. Participants were seated at round tables of eight. Jim, opening with a quick introduction, asked table groups to look into a box placed in the center of each table. The members of each group were asked to use the game pieces and follow the printed guidelines found in the box and engage in direct interaction with one another for the next twenty minutes. As group members began to converse and engage each other, Jim watched the dynamics, gathering data for feedback from the interactions. Jim knew that each person possessed within himself or herself the potential to find the best answers when afforded the space and freedom to do so. His answers could not be theirs.

Jim is an example of authentic charismatic leadership. By the end of the day, participants had direct peer feedback as well as a better sense of their own style of managing conflict. They took home concrete personal decisions for change. A major bonus, noted on the evaluation sheets, was the new friends and contacts they had made. Jim, by placing the interaction in the group, helped them draw from their own deep wells for problem solving. It is a well that will be readily accessible to them in the future when the seminar leader is only a dim memory.

Both Barbara and Jim model a graceful presence that is not tied up in ego-induced self-centeredness but a Spirit-centeredness. This new spirit helps people to take into account other people as well as themselves. It points to a larger vision of the community working together to energize a result grander than any one person could create alone.

As you seek soulful souls, your own and others', here is an affirmation to use for future thought and reflection.

Today I take the opportunity to cultivate healthy spiritual and mentoring relationships. The gift of a spiritual friend is a gift I give myself. Spiritual friends and mentors give me intimate companionship for the journey. There is much I can learn from spiritual friends and mentors even as I share my offerings with them.

I know that both giving and receiving spiritual direction entails the risk of being vulnerable; it means making the decision to trust and to be trustworthy. Even so, having or being a mentor is worth all the risk and uncertainty. Sharing experiences brings insight that otherwise would be missing in my life.

I choose mentors who are loving and wise. Our words and actions convey a mutual respect. If in years past mentors were missing from my life, I now know that God intends for me to make this life journey with companions. So I set myself free from trying to go it alone and appreciate the mentors in my life even as I mentor others.

127

=== 11 ===

What's Real and What's Not

Spiritwork: Naming reality

I t is an illusion to believe that any organization, institution, or company can hand you what you need to
fulfill your life. Leaders need to know the reality of
their organizations and institutions. Frustration
comes when we live an illusion, instead of the reality, by
asking from systems what they cannot give. Many of us
start out unrealistically believing that the organization can
meet our deepest desires.

This is true for many who become caught up in working
for the organized church. Surely, they think, within the
church they will find the identity and security they long
for. They will be valued and affirmed. They will be healthy,
wealthy (or at least have a roof over their head), and whole.
As long as they do certain things for the organization, their
needs will be met. They trust the system will take care of
them. In the church or industry, this theory usually proves
wrong.

Knowing what is real and what is not is essential to
getting through the tough times. We determine our realities

by what we allow and do not allow to exist in our lives. We define what is worthy of our time and what we will not give energy to. In this ordering process we discover truths, first about ourselves, then about others and our work organizations. We make intentional choices to define our reality so that others do not decide them for us.

What is reality? It is what we pay attention to. Reality is not something that lives out there, somehow external to us. Instead, to keep it vital, we choose to let it live within us. Our personal reality is defined by our perception of external surroundings, by what we think is real. It is determined by the energy we give to events and people in our life. We interact, believe, and collaborate with it to give it power. Personal reality is determined by the time we invest and the priority it has in our day-to-day lifestyle choices.

Perceptions of what is real and what is not differ from person to person and may change with time and experience. My reality is unique to me, and yours to you. Each person absorbs experiences differently. Two people in the same company witness a work-related incident and yet their retelling of the experience may differ completely.

What we believe is real determines, in large part, how we view ourselves and will have ramifications on the kind of leader we will be. An easy example of how self-perceptions feed our reality can be found in the story of Rajah.

Rajah is an olive-skinned, black-haired son of an Indian mother and a Euro-American father. "My parents met when my father, a consultant for a worldwide corporation, was working with a company in India, and I grew up in private schools around the world. But it wasn't a very cosmopolitan environment, even though we were living overseas; the kids in the English-speaking schools all seemed to be perfectly blonde, blue-eyed replicas of the actors I saw in old fifties movies. I felt ashamed of my dark complexion; I stopped playing outdoors—to my mother's horror—when I was thirteen, because I was

*afraid the sun would only make me darker. I didn't
want to look foreign and exotic; I wanted to look like
everyone else in my school. The other kids even used
ethnic slurs when they teased me. Frankly, I hated
everything about my looks."*

At thirty-three, Rajah manages a computer supply store
in Manhattan, where his appearance is completely unre-
markable in a city of hundreds of racial and ethnic groups.
"I look around me," he says, "and I know in my head that
there's nothing at all wrong with the way I look. But deep
down, another reality broods—pain and shame. I've never
quite gotten over the idea that I'd prefer to look like
someone else."

Most persons grow up with some sense of inadequacy,
a reality that gradually changes as we mature into adulthood. Changing our view of reality is not easy, but it can
be done and gets easier as time goes by. We never forget
those first perceptions, but we can learn another way to
relate and think about ourselves. We can choose to live life
through a different reality.

If my reality includes believing myself to be a person of
worth, just as other people are also valued, then I will live
in consistent, respectful, caring ways. If I do not like myself
or see other people only as vehicles to meet my needs, then
daily interactions will be disrespectful and uncaring. The
spirit condition of our souls is inseparably intertwined with
our behavior. We live out the state of our spirit in every
facet of life. It determines our behavior toward our family
and friends at home and colleagues and associates at work.
A healthy reality is one that values all of life and each
member in it.

What's the Reality of Our Organizations?

Ilene, a foreman at a local factory, shares her story:

When our factory was bought out by a larger corporation, everyone was on edge. We didn't know what the change would mean. The new managers came in with a flourish and lots of promises. This immediately put the workers at ease. Everyone was upbeat. I, as a lower-level foreman, was relieved I could share some good news with the workers after living for so many weeks of tension on the factory floor. The promises included on-site child care, an exercise room complete with aerobic classes, and profit sharing. It seemed like this new management really cared and would do good by the employees.

As the weeks wore on, the reality became clear. Child care was provided, from nine to five. Factory workers' shifts started at seven. The exercise room opened at 5:00 P.M., long after the wage earners had left for home. It became apparent that the benefits were for the salaried executive staff. The books continued to be "fixed" so a profit never appeared.

I found myself stuck in the middle, questioning the new management and apologizing to the workers. The services were on paper, but in reality they didn't exist. I soon learned that this show of nonexistent benefits had been made to fulfill requirements for a local bank loan. There was never any intention to care for the factory workers.

Selling Our Souls to the Company Store

In addition to creating illusions of care, systems have strange ways of keeping us in line. How do they do this? They give us the illusion that our good name and well-being rest in them. They have an investment in wanting us to believe that as part of the existing structure we will be safe and cared for. Without them we will become less of who we are. I would guess that corporations, companies, and

131

institutions, with or without intention, keep employees in line through these means.

My maternal grandfather, Jacob Griffith, was a Welsh miner who began to work the coal tunnels of Pennsylvania at the age of ten. Always needing more than his weekly paycheck allowed, he found that the lyrics of the coal mining song rang true, "I owe my soul to the company store." The company owned and controlled not only the store but also the schools, the housing, and even the medical care. With eight hungry mouths to feed and no formal education, Jacob felt he had no other choice but to enter the dark death pits each dawn. I have few memories of him except quick flashes of his wretched sickness and violent, bloody coughing spells. He may have held on to a piece of his soul but gave his life. Jacob died of black lung disease at the too-young age of fifty-two.

We, too, ask if we are selling our souls to the company store. For some there is little choice. So we submit our days to an all-knowing boss who supplies our needs and an institution that gives us the illusion of being well cared for. Of course, there are a few things asked of us in return. This seems reasonable. We expect it. We give forty hours a week, more or less, and produce the desired product, whatever it is. A few other "little" demands are also asked of us.

1. *We are asked to deny our own experience when it tells us that what we are doing isn't working.* No one wants to admit that what he or she has given a whole life to doing isn't working. So the longer the invested interest, the easier it is to keep workers playing along.

2. *We are asked not to worry about present circumstances, but to believe the promise that things will get better.* This paints the picture that things are all right, even when they aren't. And even if they aren't, it really doesn't matter. Buying into the denial process of the organized structure, focusing on the future, keeps everyone from doing the hard work of figuring out what's wrong today. It is an elaborate set up of denial that keeps the status quo in place.

Jill, a young executive, shared these just-named insights with Henry, an older associate. "You're wrong," the associate replied. Jill was surprised at his defensiveness. "You are young and simply haven't seen the company the way I have." Jill knew that she had lived enough years in the corporate structure to know her own experience. She also understood what Henry was doing. In order to maintain his view of reality and protect the institution, the older associate sought to find some fault in Jill or in her reasoning. In this case, he cited her youth and inexperience. In this way, Henry could also dismiss what she was saying.

Instead of shrinking away, which Jill would have done at one time, she came back. "You are right," she said. "I am comparatively young." (Jill was forty-one, Henry sixty-three.) "But, that does not mean my perceptions are incorrect or invalid."

Then, to show Jill where she was wrong, Henry began to soothingly speak about the times the organization had come through for him—the time his daughter had become sick and colleagues took up a collection to help with medical bills and the flowers that arrived when his father died. Jill added bits of her own story, recalling the check the employee aid society had sent when she demolished her car, the women who gave her an after-work babyshower, and the cards that came when a family member died.

Then it dawned on Jill. She and Henry were not talking about the institution. Instead, they were citing examples of caring individuals who happened to be members of the institution.

Clearly, these persons' actions were being absorbed by the system and used to validate itself in order to perpetuate the organization. It is easy to buy in to this denial, knowing things are really terrible, but hoping that maybe, just maybe things are changing and it will be different next time.

Anne Wilson Schaef, in her book *When Society Becomes an Addict,* paints a realistic picture as she talks about organized religion. "There is no group in our society more adept at this process than the church, for which one of the major premises is that of eternal life. That promise keeps us actively involved in pleasing the church and doing what it tells us to do. We ignore the present because we are assured salvation and a brighter future. We can look to a time when our worries and cares will fall away and be replaced by bliss—so why change today?" Although Schaef is talking about religious institutions, she could easily be speaking of many places of employment.

Companies no longer feel responsible to employees or their families. Health insurance and pension plans are not offered by many employers. There is less chance of advancement in the old sense of the word, as companies struggle to exist and adapt in a swiftly changing culture. At one time we looked to career advancement to fulfill our ego needs. Now we cannot look to an office as proof of our value. In truth, many of us fear that we are only one step away from becoming the next bag lady.

Do you believe that if you could just figure out the system and your place in it everything would be all right? Are you awakening to see the "rescue fantasy" for what it is? As you begin to understand the limitations and assets of your organization as they really are, you have decisions and choices to make. I've listed three for consideration.

- Door Number One: Stay and become numb.
- Door Number Two: Stay with integrity.
- Door Number Three: Get out.

I am going to change the sequence and save door number two for last. This is not because it is the final or better choice, nor does it infer ranking. Each of us has chosen one of these doors at some time. Circumstances necessitate such choices. As we choose our path, we recognize how each choice relates to the Spirit. The reason why I reorder the doors is simply because those persons who plan to stay within the system and remain spiritually healthy will need the most help.

Door Number One: Stay and Become Numb

You can allow others to make decisions for you based on what they think is best. But do not expect them to make these decisions in your best interest. They will make the decision, but in their own best interest and for the ongoing maintenance of the organization. Of course, letting others make the decision releases you from anxiety and responsibility, but the price for such *laissez-faire* management is high.

To remain with door number one, you will need to anesthetize yourself to continue to function. In essence, you sell your soul. The sad truth is that people choose to live in denial and numbness when the truth is too painful. You'll be a valuable employee, since organizations and institutions have a strong investment in keeping employees numb to preserve the current balance. It is easier to manipulate numb workers than aware, sometimes angry, ones.

Door Number Three: Get Out

You may choose door number three and get out of a sick organization. You may decide it is the only way you can stay healthy and Spirit-centered. It feels scary to risk leaving. But it is even riskier to lose your soul. The only way to find health may be to leave the system. It may be necessary to get out. The truth is that many healthy people are leaving unhealthy organizations. A special note: These numb, sick institutions have a way of weeding out some of their healthiest people.

"When I step back and take the long view of most structures, organizations, and hierarchies that are in

*place, when I gaze at the business offices and build-
ings that have been constructed, I don't see one—not
one building, budget, or committee, not any of it that
I would have done that way," Martin Wolitz expressed to his colleague Roberto Santos. Looking
perplexed, Roberto asked, "But if we don't do this
(meaning attending all the meetings, continuing the
work to maintain the existing structures, climb the
ladder), then what will we do?"*

Martin was right. Our whole life is tied up in doing this.
We get so entrenched in doing all *this* that we end up
putting our true spiritual power on the shelf. Think of all
the time and energy we expend maintaining structures
when we could be using our potential in creative, life-build-
ing ways.

Sometimes places of employment are so immoral, im-
poverished, and spiritless that we have no choice but to
walk away. To remain entrenched in them is a form of living
death. There is no excuse for giving away your life to a
system. It is the only life you have. No paycheck, benefits
package, or pension plan can replace it. If you cannot live
out your destiny within the corporation, then you may
need to get out. Pause and reflect on three questions:

1. What burns within you and gives your life meaning?
2. What gives you passion to live?
3. What restores your energy and calls forth the best that
   is within you?

When you cultivate your deepest desires and longings, you
sense you are living in truth and are fully alive. You know
that you are living the Spirit's will for your life. Life has
meaning. As you work on what is most precious to you,
the answers will align themselves with your heart's desire.

What do those who choose to leave unhealthy organizations do? Some begin their own businesses. Others find
new places to work. There are no easy answers. That is
why most of us try to function within door number two.

If you have already been irreversibly sucked into the undertow of your organization's disease and chosen door number one, chances are you probably aren't still reading this book. If you are still reading this chapter, that's a good sign. If your decision was door number two, hold on and get ready for a long roller coaster ride.

Door Number Two: Stay with Integrity

In the blockbuster movie *A League of Their Own*, a woman's professional baseball league is created to fill the vacancy left by young men's service in World War II. In what I thought was the best scene of the movie, the main character, the best player, is packed and ready to leave the rough and tumble life of major league baseball. The coach pleadingly asks why she is leaving right at the critical moment of the season. She emotionally responds, "It just got too hard!" To which the coach exclaims, "It's suppose to be hard. If it wasn't hard everyone would do it. The hard is what makes it great!" To remain in the system is hard—no ifs, ands, or buts about it! You will need stamina and endurance to make it for the long haul.

In choosing door number two, you face the joys and accomplishments as well as the hurts and disappoint-ments of the system you choose to work in. No organization is all good or all bad. Most corporations have departments and branches that are healthy as well as offices and bureaus that are unhealthy. We may be naive to think "the grass is greener" somewhere else. It may be, but then again it may not. Whatever the reality, we have chosen to stay.

Along with endurance to stay, you need to be inwardly honest with yourself and face the system for the reality it is. Most systems are like living organisms. They have a life of their own. As much as we hate to admit it, they are imperfect because they are run by imperfect persons like us. They experience good days and bad as well as both up and down times. We need to prepare our spirits for the hard times and keep reasonable expectations. What's reason-able? Only we can define what to us is reasonable. We all have varying limitations. One person's idea of what is reasonable may not be another's. You must decide.

Survival in some systems, business organizations, and institutions is like living in the belly of the beast. To remain in a sick system, you need to set new boundaries. Remember, a business is not family. They do not own you, and you are not tied genetically together forever. You are not owned by any system. View yourself as a free agent working in the system, but not of it.

Some stay and survive by moving into arenas of the organization where they are less affected by the craziness. In a few cases nonhierarchical subsets of people can exist within a hierarchical corporate structure. Others continue to make across-the-board moves, electing not to enter top management. India's one-time Prime Minister Indira Gandhi is credited with this humorous advise, "My grandfather once told me that there were two kinds of people: those who do the work and those who take credit. He told me to try to be in the first group; there was much less competition." It is advice to heed.

You Can Do It!

A main concern is to take care of yourself and remain attuned to your spiritual needs.

Stay alert so you will not be drawn into the sickness. To remain centered and confident, watch for tell-tale signs that you are overreaching. Sick systems are often workaholic organizations and will entice you to take on more and more by dangling prizes for this behavior. Overreaching our capabilities causes overwhelming stress and acute anxiety. Become your own expert on unhealthy organizations by reading two authors who have done substantial research. Anne Wilson Schaef, author of *When Society Becomes an Addict,* and Diane Fassel, author of *Working Ourselves to Death,* together wrote *The Addictive Organization,* a trilogy that is a "must read."

A few other guidelines: Stay firm on values that are not negotiable. Don't sugarcoat your position or the subject, even if it makes you unpopular with more conservative or liberal persons. A colleague patiently explained her unswerving stand on a controversial decision to her associates. "I've sat down and done the soul searching," she said. "I can't change my position. I wouldn't respect myself if I did."

As we stop working in ways that didn't work then and don't work now, we have energy to create new images. Take care that as you work in new ways you don't signal the established management where to build up a double wall of resistance. This only makes the already difficult work of reform even harder. Working against and resisting established structures can take away energy needed for the new vision. It also validates the established management by giving them your attention. We do not need to set ourselves up against existing power constructs and authority figures. To do this is the equivalent of the battered spouse giving attention to the abuser. It only eggs the abuser on to be more abusive. These actions also tend to rob us of the energy we could invest in creative, life-giving ways.

Many systems and structures, perhaps along with the one where you work, are sinful and need to be redeemed. Yet, to continue pointing the finger at the systems that oppress, putting ourselves in the victim role, does not help. When I warn about not going up against the organization, I am not saying that the system will be any less oppressive or that we will be any less disenfranchised. The system was sick when you came, and it will be sick when you leave. The organization was well when you came, and it will be well when you leave. It is not up to you to fix it.

The unhealthy organization seems to be most people's experience. Are corporate structures inherently "unhealthy"? One co-worker told me, "I have yet to talk to someone who is working for a 'Spirit-filled' organization." But there are such people within organizations. We need to seek out "Spirit-filled" people within our places of work. They are there. I always find it a mystery that these people surface as I strive to live and work in healthy ways.

Intentionally identifying and connecting with them is one strategy for survival.

Each person needs to see and understand his or her part in the play. Sometimes this is difficult. How do we know when the organization is growing more unhealthy and when we are the ones unable to respond in healthy ways? How can we tell when problems are our own, related to our limitations, or outside ourselves? It is not always easy to know, in times of downsizing and hierarchical management.

Jennifer is a "lead" nurse in a large medical practice that was recently taken over by a hospital. Jennifer has always worked hard to make things better wherever she is. Others turn to her for leadership. Jennifer suggests improvements in handling medical files, scheduling clients, and rotating nurses. She has always been lifted up as a model of how to care for patients. She is exemplary in her ability to build working doctor-nurse teams. Now she explains she is very close to door number one.

"It seems that the top managers of the practice are so distant from the day-to-day work that there is little connection between management decisions and the reality of what needs to be done. I can't just turn off my natural impulse to help make things better. I'm constantly frustrated in my attempts because my staff turns over so often. We are extremely understaffed, and there is little I can do about it with the control isolated at the top."

Like Jennifer, sometimes the most we can do is to look and see, as clearly as possible, the reality of our organizations and then make our choices. Will you be absorbed into the existing system, or will you work for new models? Will you be co-opted by the institution you work in or create a new reality? Will you be an agent for change, or will you be changed by the existing institutional environment? Will you be part of the future shock or the future hope? It all depends on your spirit.

CONCLUSION
Becoming an Affirmation Mystic

My spouse and I have experienced all the ins and outs, ups and downs of married life. Some mornings I wake up with this man beside me, look at his gentle, sleeping countenance, and think I must be the luckiest woman in the world. Other mornings I awaken wondering who this unshaven stranger is lying next to me and if I can ask him when he plans to leave. It is on these latter mornings of doubts that I try to recall why I said, "I do." I search my memory to conjure up evidences of earlier romance. I remember our original vision of how wonderful life together would be. In our ideal life together, we would never fight or disagree, always be respectful, and never embarrass the other. Together we would make the world a better place to live. Although we now face the reality of our union, this is the "original vision" that we still see for ourselves. It is the hope of all we can be. At times it helps our marriage commitment continue when we'd rather opt out.

Our original vision of life generates memories we hark back to during the rough times. Remembrances draw out our fullest potential. Original vision is the vehicle that joins what we can see today with what we hope for tomorrow, to arrive at a new destination.

141

Conclusion

The Bottom Line

Most books on leadership have a chapter on vision. This book is no exception. Companies and corporations are spending inordinate amounts of time, money, and energy paying professional consultants to help them construct vision statements. Yet, vision, to the Spirit-filled leader, no matter how helpful and defining for us or for our organization, cannot be held up as the ultimate prize. No matter how perfect the vision, it is not the pot of gold at the end of the rainbow. Our visions, both personal and corporate, come and go. They change with times and life circumstances.

The truth is that no vision will hold you in your deepest, darkest hour. No conjured-up vision, no matter how grand, will sustain you in your moment of death. So what is the bottom line if it isn't vision? *The bottom line is relationship—with ourselves, with others, and with God.*

• *In relationship with ourselves*, we are attentive to our own journey. We establish a true inner authority that comes from our souls. This authority is not dependent on scholastic degrees, titles, or professional status. Instead, we operate out of a free place from within. We open ourselves to live our experiences to their fullest and deepest potential. We care for our spiritual well-being, thereby laying the foundation to live intimately with ourselves. In relationship with ourselves, we are soulful people who are vulnerable, caring, and growing.

We recognize our own needs and the right for our will to exist and have inner power. Remember, the powers of this world do not have an investment in our living with an authority from within. For companies and corporations whose first concern is meeting management goals, sales profits, and imminent deadlines, the cost is too high. These systems know that free people claiming their own power seek truth and not control. They seek to build the cosmos into the image of God. That's dangerous stuff!

• *In relationship with others*, we treat persons with the respect and civility that is rightfully theirs as persons of sacred worth. Each person we encounter is a unique "pearl of great price." As we walk the road with them, we strive to be fully present with each person we greet. As one spiritual teacher once reminded me, "Remember that we are not here to see through each other, but to see each other through."

• *In our relationship with God,* ultimately it all comes down to our personal encounter with the One who has tenderly held us since our first breath, walked gently beside us in the hard times, and will finally be the truth that cradles us in our moment of death. We are intricately connected to our Divine Center. The author of life bids us to be in authentic relationship with ourselves, with others, and, therefore, with the Divine of All Life who is the original "original vision."

Holy Habits for the Long Haul

We already know the lesson. We learned it the hard way. And the debris of broken friendships and lost loves litters our lives to remind us: *It takes hard work and stick-with-it commitment to sustain relationship.* Anyone who has ever lived in covenant relationship, whether it be with family, spouse, partners, or colleagues will attest to this truth. Relationships can only be sustained in love lived with perseverance and disciple—holy habits. We continue healthy relationships as we give them the time they deserve and put in place lifestyle practices that continue to strengthen our commitment to ourselves and to others. In all of this, we live in ways that point to an authority greater than ourselves. We point to the core meaning of life: God, the original vision of the Spirit.

Keeping Original Vision

I am deeply distressed when I encounter people who have lost the rich original vision of the Spirit. Where did it go? Original vision, when alive and well, leads us into wondrous possibilities and the glorious passion of living.

This vision has always required a rich and full imagination grounded in hope. It is through hope—that which is not seen, that connects the spiritual and temporal, the invisible and the visible, the earthly and the heavenly. As leaders, we want technical explanations, scientific information, and the latest computer technology at our fingertips. But this will not be enough. Even with all these in place, we still need two essential gifts: vision and hope. They live, breathe, and have their being—together.

Many of us have been so busy "getting in" and "fitting in" that we've lost track of the original vision of our vocation. Ask yourself these questions:

• Has your original vision of leadership faded, and with it your dreams?
• Have you forgotten the hopes and aspirations you held at the beginning?
• Have you grown afraid, relinquishing the hopes of change to live instead in the safety of what is known and controllable?

As the essence of who we are is stifled or systematically depleted, we can loose sight of the dream. We can easily become robots of the status quo and guardians of stagnation.

In our workaday world, it is the original vision that allows us to stay in the system when we'd rather quit. It is this vision that keep us on the straight and narrow. It directs us in the right when we'd rather do wrong. It is a vision for leaders who swing from the ropes into the unknown, but who live in the realistic hope that the next rope will appear. We can be empowered to claim our vision and be a stronghold of healing in the belly of the beast.

Fad diets, exercise regimens, headache remedies, and even leadership seminars have an investment to keep you believing that there is a secret formula, sure-fire steps, seven habits, or a pocketful of miracles, that, if followed precisely, will put you on the road to successful living. I must tell you the truth: I have no magical formula that will make you stay centered and lead in Spirit-filled ways. It takes more than pious, highfalutin talk to be a Spirit-energized leader. Instead, it requires consistent, persistent action to spiritually maintain yourself for the difficult role of leadership. I have eight basic daily living practices that I strive to keep in my life; they may surprise you in their simplicity.

1. *Move and keep moving.* I use exercise to cut stress and energize all my senses. I walk. My walks around the neighborhood are both exercise and a chance to think things over in low-pressure surroundings. It's not a competitive sport. I usually walk alone, but enjoy companionship when my husband or a friend joins me on my daily journey. Sometimes I take a book and stroll more leisurely about. (If you try this, watch out for curbs and potholes. A friend of mine fell in one doing just this!) I like hearing the birds, seeing the trees, and feeling alive. It is my time alone, as I literally walk away from it all. I can reflect on the day and my relationships. I pray thanksgivings and concerns. When I feel stressed and don't exercise, it is like peddling and braking at the same time.

2. *Get down; get dirty.* Gardening is exercise as well as an earthy meditation. All morning I may sit at my computer or spend a hard day at work, but in the afternoon or early evening working with my flowers and herbs connects me with the simple goodness of the earth. It's heartwarming to play with beautiful living things. It connects me to the present, and my lists of things to do melt away. A statue of Saint Francis, the brother who lived a gentle life with all creation, sits in my garden to remind me to respect and count as sacred all living things on God's good earth. Perhaps you connect with nature in a different way—camping, hiking, sitting under a tree. Time spent "with nature" replenishes our souls.

3. *Immerse yourself with calm.* About four times a year I literally take a day apart. It is a quiet retreat away from my office, home, and routine. In a small community of like-minded persons, stories and prayers are shared. Sometimes I speak, and sometimes I remain silent. Either is accepted. We break bread together. Undisturbed silence

is at the center of the day. Reflection, meditation, and prayer fill the designated hours.

Each night I take a simple bath at the end of my day, each day. This relieves tension and tight muscles. I fill the tub to the brim, sink in, and close my eyes for fifteen minutes. It's the one door in our house you can lock without feeling guilty. Telephone messages are taken, and no one dares knock. If my muscles haven't relaxed by the time I get out, it is a sure sign that I need to reevaluate my schedule and realign my life.

4. *Enjoy the music.* I have a CD player in my office, so when things get just too stressful I close my door and turn it on. I do not always play quiet, meditative music either. I like swaying around to Van Morrison and singing with Barbra Streisand or Tony Bennett—not a sight you would want your "higher ups" to witness. It's my way of playing in the middle of the day. I don't have to plan ahead. This swift change of tempo brings life back into focus, and the insignificant troubles of the day melt away.

5. *Read, so you know you're not alone.* I read the newspaper in the morning and an article or chapter before I turn off my light at night. In between I read interesting books for my work. Novels and poetry, how-to books, and biographies are all part of my collection. We already discussed the idea of incorporating devotional and meditative readings in an earlier chapter. Remember to read from the holy books. I read to stay informed with the world and to expand myself.

6. *Laugh, laugh, and laugh!* I read the comics and political cartoons every morning. These help me keep things in line and add the touch of not taking myself too seriously. I laugh with my kids. We go to an amusement park at least once a summer just for the fun of it. Most of all, I enjoy laughing with my friends. Once a year I combine three of my favorite things—music, dance, and laughter—and with a group of friends celebrate that we've made it through another year. It's like it's everyone's birthday all at once!

7. *Keep priorities written down.* I carry a journal with me. In it I record the tasks I do, notes to myself, ideas for

speeches and books, thoughts, reflections and prayers, and my list of priorities. I keep my priorities front and center. I list six priorities, no more. When being pulled in different directions, I am tempted to give everything the same priority. This doesn't work. When I keep my top six front and center, it's easier to say that word—*no*. That one word reduces stress and returns my sense of what's important in life.

8. *Carpe diem. Seize the day!* Live in this present moment of eternity. Every once in while I live through a day as if it were my last. This helps me to sort out who and what is truly important to me. It also helps me to say the thank yous, I love yous, and words of appreciation that I've been storing up. I let go of resentments against co-workers, friends, and family. Most important, I release the worry about what happened yesterday or what may happen in the future. Today is it. So live it to the max!

Vision Expansion

I pray that what I have shared about leadership helps you as much as this process of writing has aided me. Spirit-centered leadership is still a vision that awaits realization. Together we can write the next chapter. This vision we're writing is not the standard, "Where do you want to be five years from now?" Becoming engrossed in only our own agenda and not seeing other people's needs or the bigger picture of our place in God's world leads to sickness and sorrow instead of joy. Spiritual leaders contribute to life even as they care for themselves. Leaders who wish to lead by the Spirit within must hold a vision that encompasses all people and the whole of creation with gentleness and grace.

It is not enough for leaders to be well trained and educated, highly principled, earnestly moral individuals. All of these attributes are important and valuable, but they are not what is at the heart of Spirit-centered leadership. Without the Spirit, leaders will be little more than sociologists, psychologists, and social workers trying to intellectually analyze to manipulate an end. Without the Spirit, leaders may still be good managers, enablers, facilitators, encouragers, and role models helping others find their ways through the stresses and strains of the working life. They may even make small contributions to find solutions for the troubles of our time. But none of these abilities is the basis of who we are meant to be.

Instead, the spiritual leader's reality of self is filled with the desire to live in the divine's presence. In this expanding reality, we hear God's voice, feel God's presence, and taste fully the joyful anticipation of all that can be and is yet to be. When our leadership is centered in the divine source of life we are able to remain strong but not rigid, assertive but not offensive, and gentle with people but not wishy washy. It is from this source that we find the wisdom and courage to address whatever challenges arise.

Frenzied, disquieting voices of the world will try to make us deaf to the gentle, soft, caring call of the Spirit. But it is our task, as Spirit-led people, to stand with others as they too hear the beckoning voice, to work and lead in new ways. Spiritual leader Henri Nouwen talks about his own journey, which led him to be in touch with the movement of God's Spirit within. In his book *In the Name of Jesus: Reflections on Christian Leadership*, Nouwen so lovingly says it for us, "God is a God of the present and reveals to those who are willing to listen carefully to the moment in which they live the steps they are to take toward the future." Our part requires us to listen, to invite others and ourselves to enter into a deeply spiritual formation that involves all of who we are, mind, body and heart.

Our sacred task is to discern, name, and announce, from moment to moment and day to day, the ways in which God is in our midst. Our first job is to discover the presence of the holy within ourselves and our community, leading people out of captivity to a new home. For leaders to be truly effective in this new time, they must move from what they think in their own minds and intellects is right to the mystical acknowledgment of the spiritual power that lies beyond themselves.

Conclusion

Affirmation Mystics

Howard Thurman, the great theologian and philosopher, called himself an "affirmation mystic." His mysticism, rooted in affirmation, led him to love people and to work for justice. We, too, as Spirit-focused leaders, centered in original vision, can aspire to be affirmation mystics with our identities deeply rooted in the Spirit's love. Our life is dominated not by our need for approval, our self-centered ego, or a struggle for scarcity-modeled power. Instead, our identity is firmly grounded in the Spirit. Living in hope, we stifle the voices of fatalism, oppression, and defeatist attitudes and actions. We live as agents of affirmation, seeking always what is true and right and good.

Here is a final affirmation reflection. I write it for us to use as together we lean into the future:

As an affirmation mystic, I make strong choices. I avoid beliefs and feelings that throw me back into self-defeating patterns. I take the needed time and energy to sustain intimate relationships and care for my own garden. I refuse to cultivate the insanity of institutions and organizations that are unhealthy and spiritless. I find the contentment that leads to a Spirit-centered life. Finally I know that my life is dependent upon my perseverance to study and meditate, to have time for renewal and prayerful reflection.

Grabbing the rope, we change the world even as we change ourselves. Seeing through the surface world in which we live, we dive down deeper to claim the forces that shape us. As we swing out over the rim, daring the abyss and stepping beyond the limits, we lead God's people home.

A vision without Spirit is hopeless.

A spirit without a vision is impossible.

But with vision rooted in the Spirit's power that lies beyond—all things are enfolded in hope and possibility!

149